Native American Adult Coloring Book

This Coloring book belongs to:

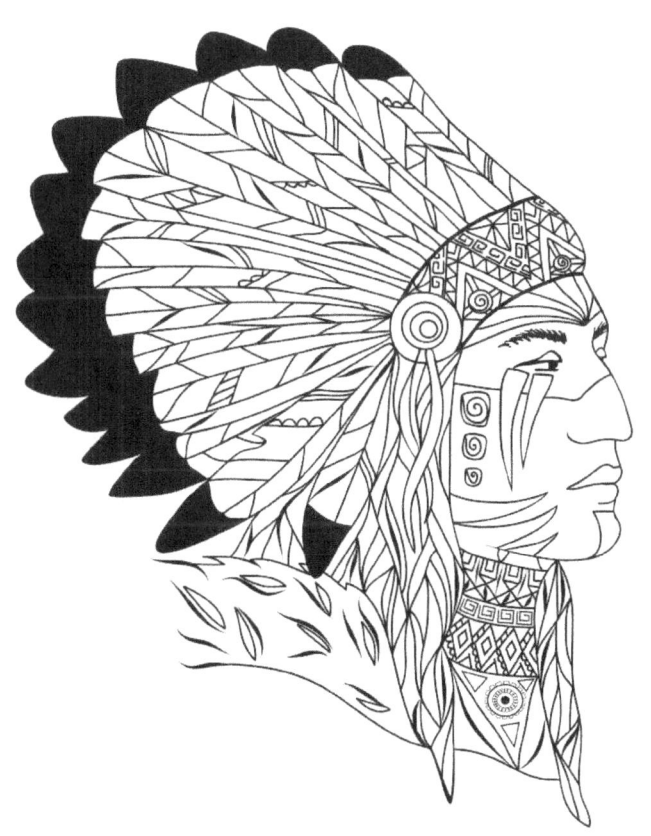

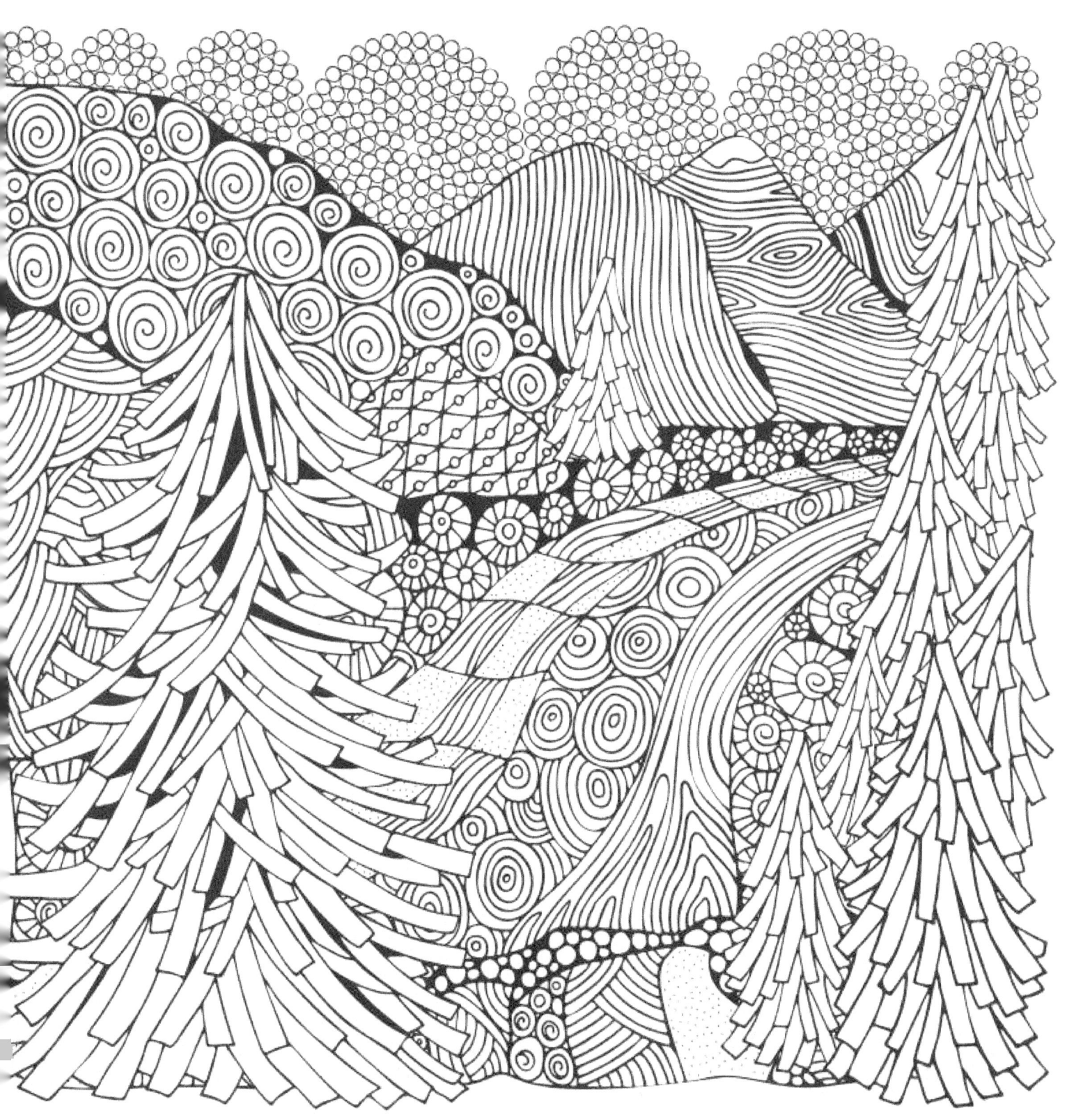

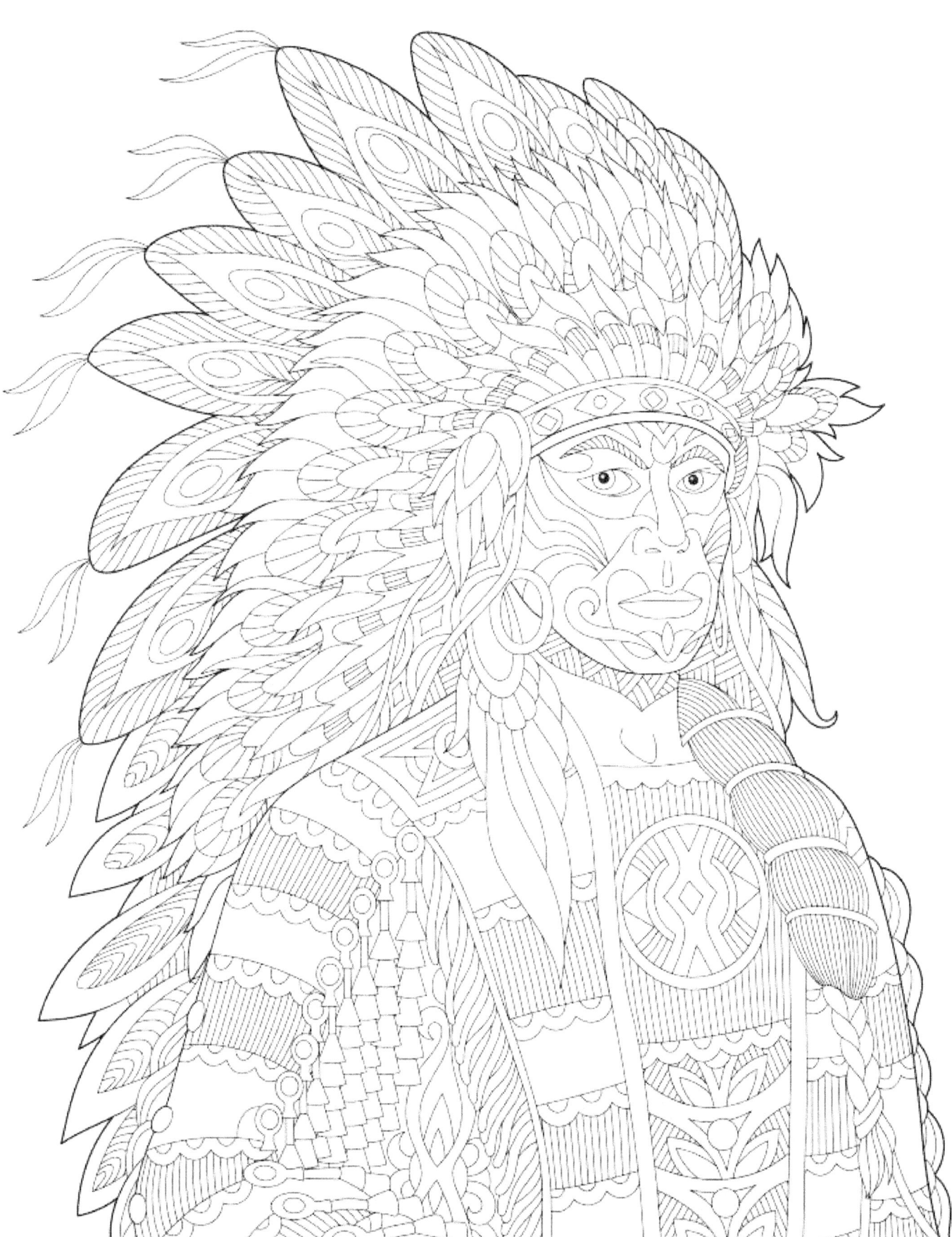

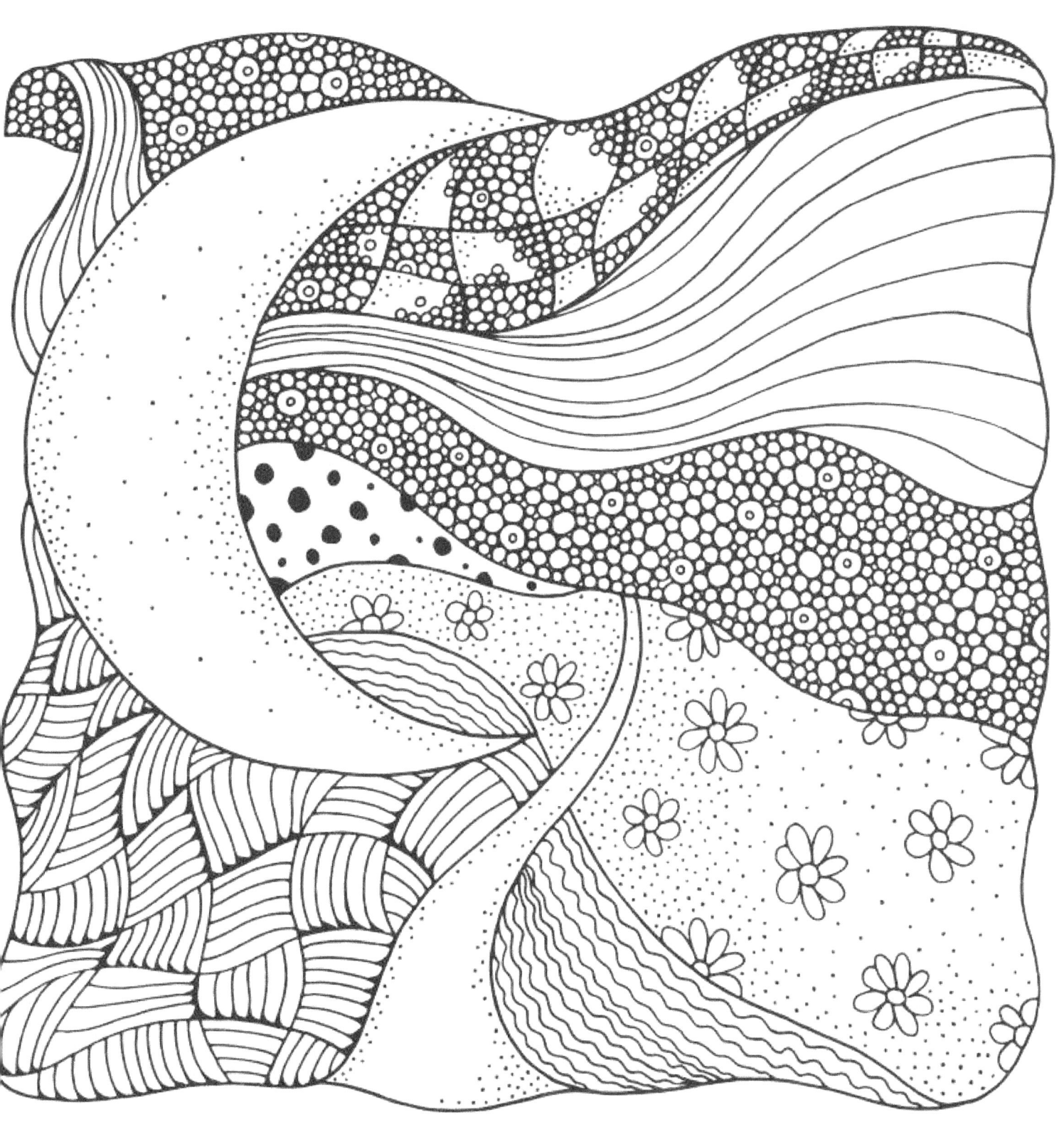

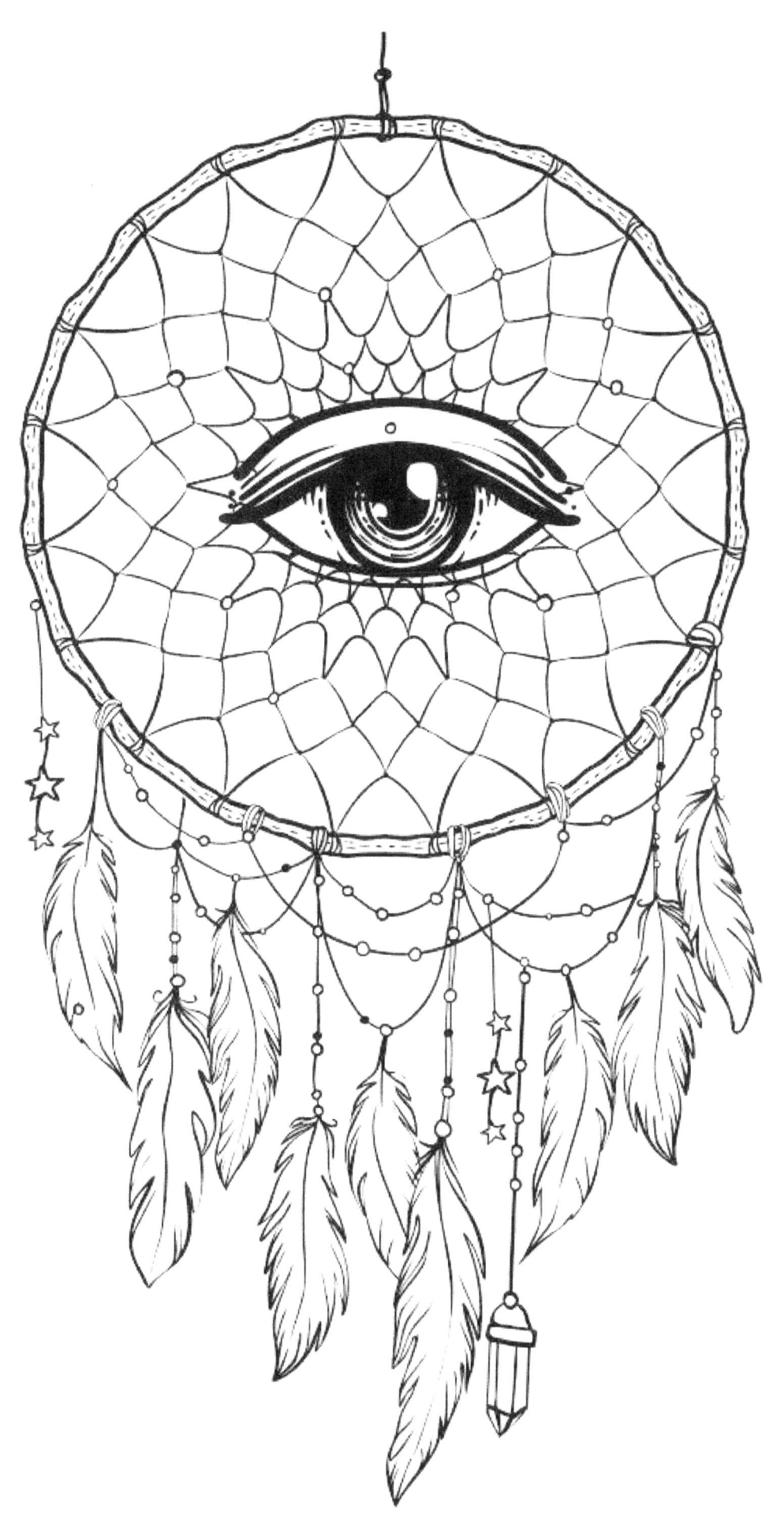

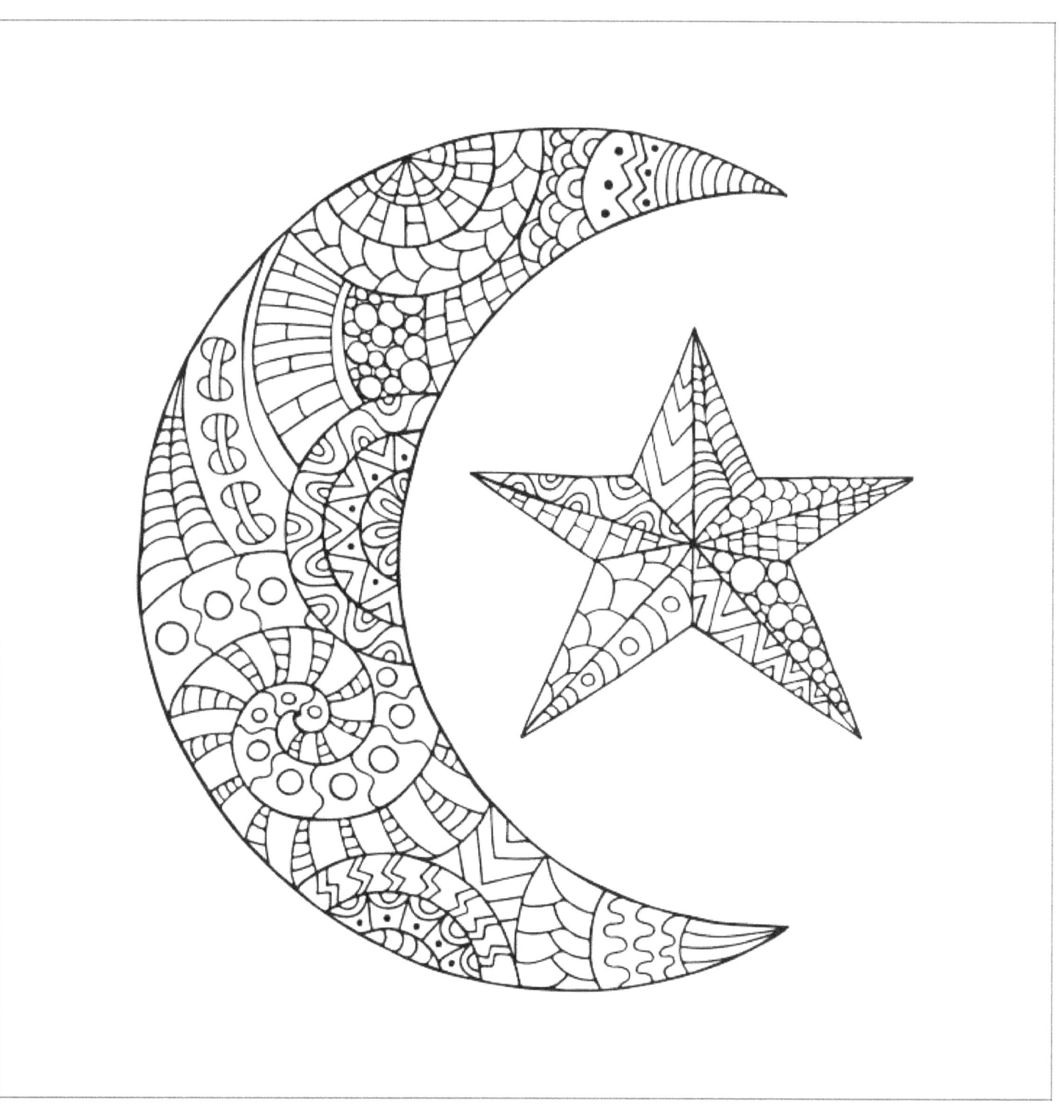

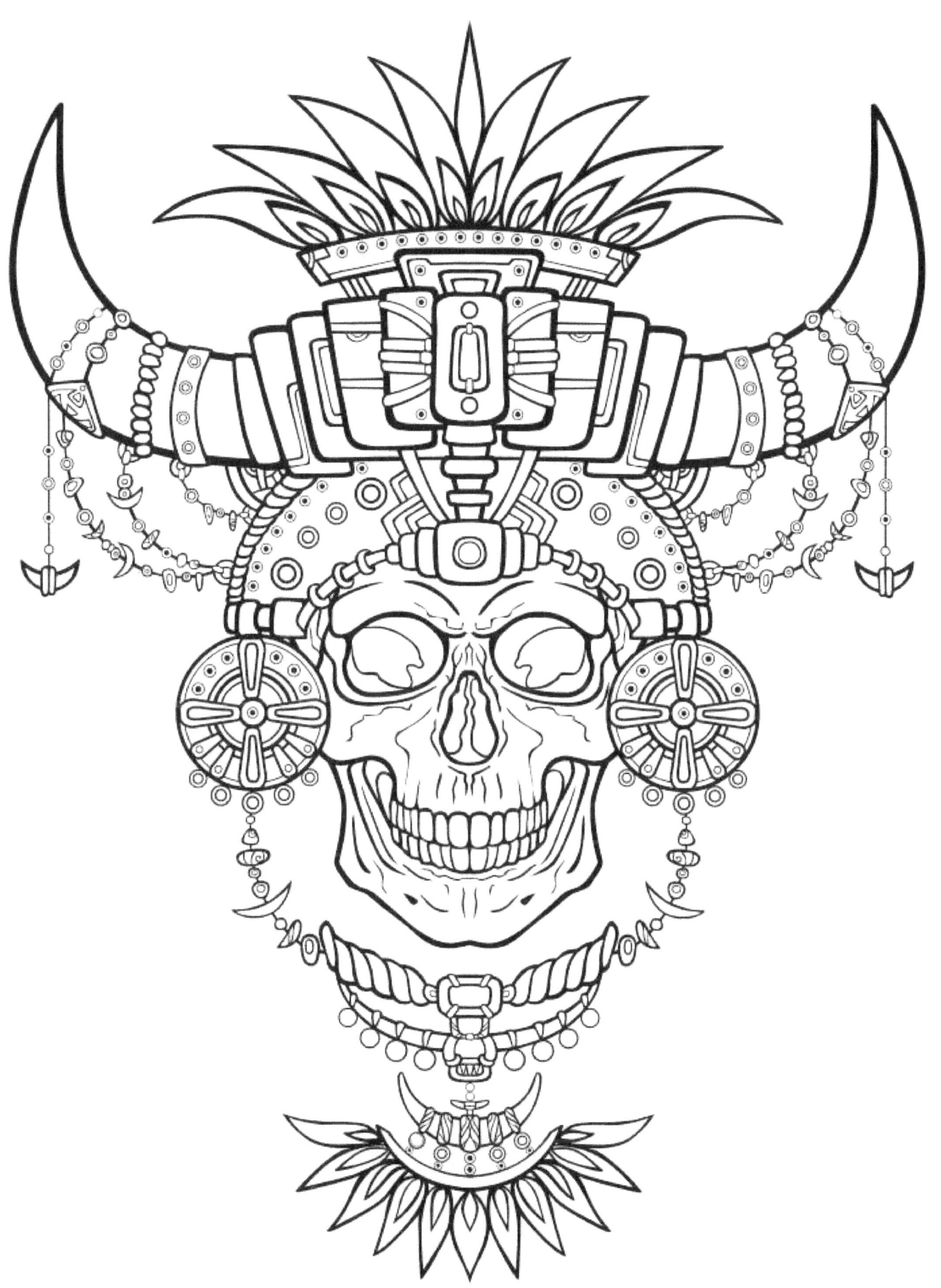

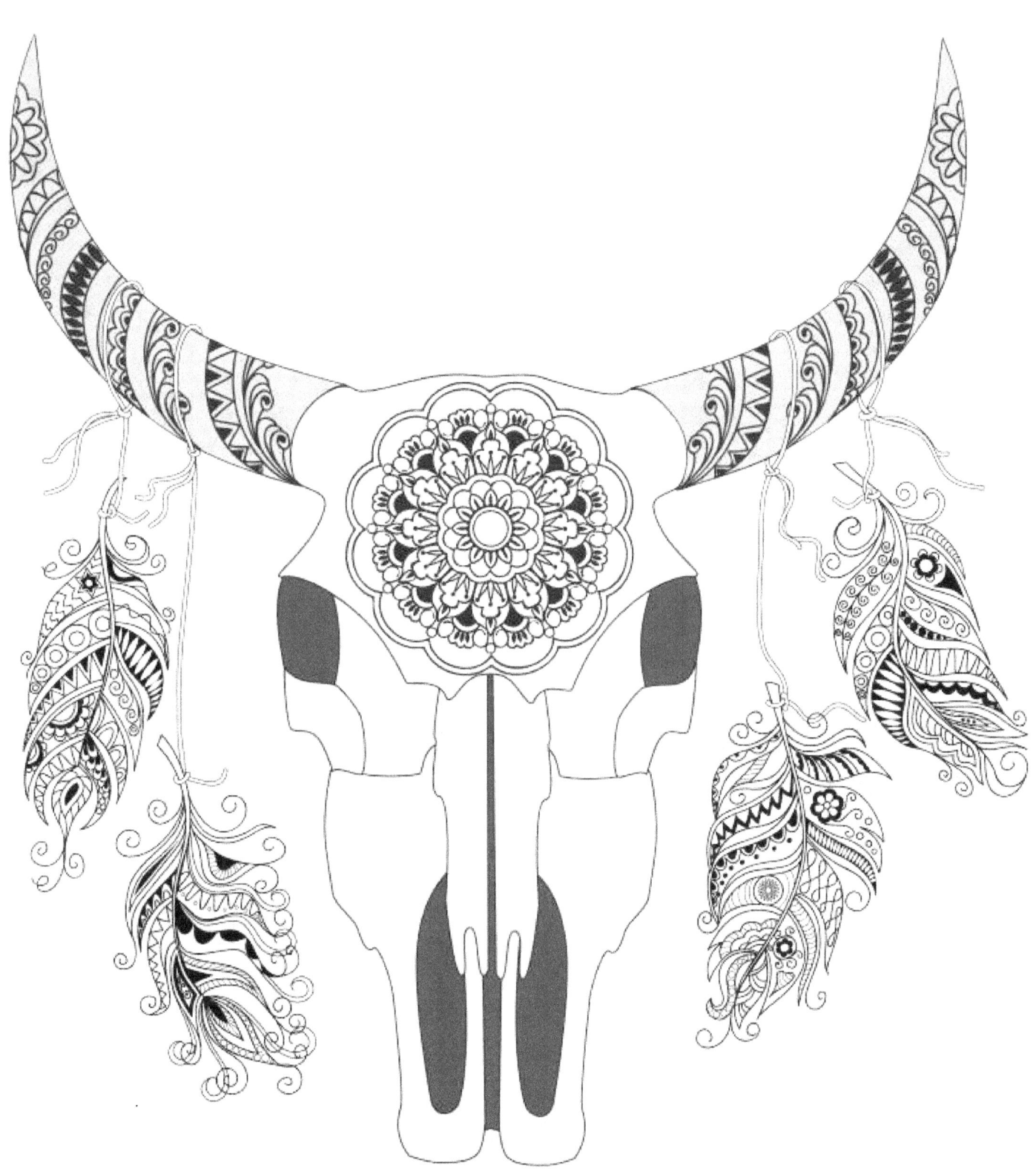

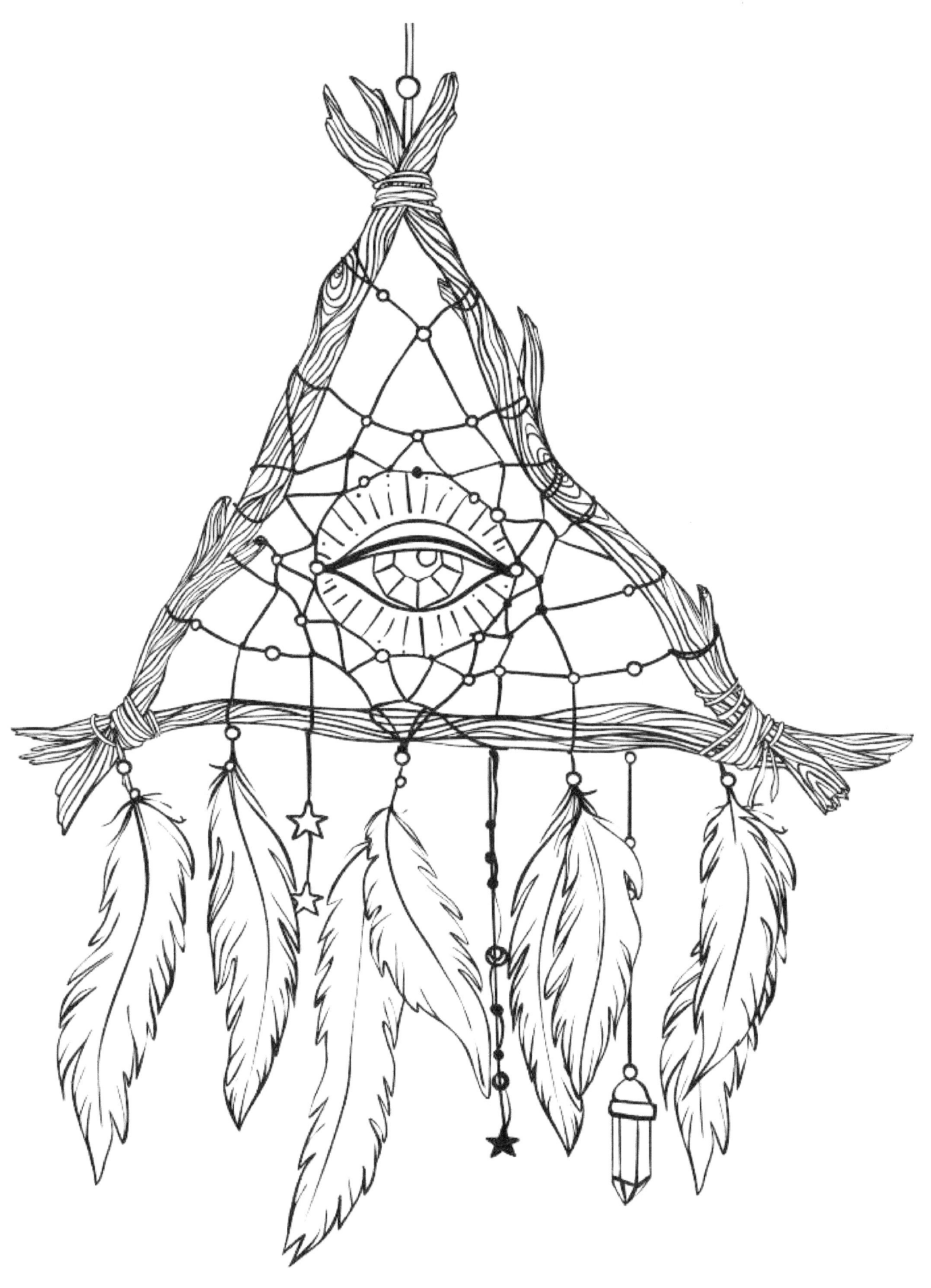

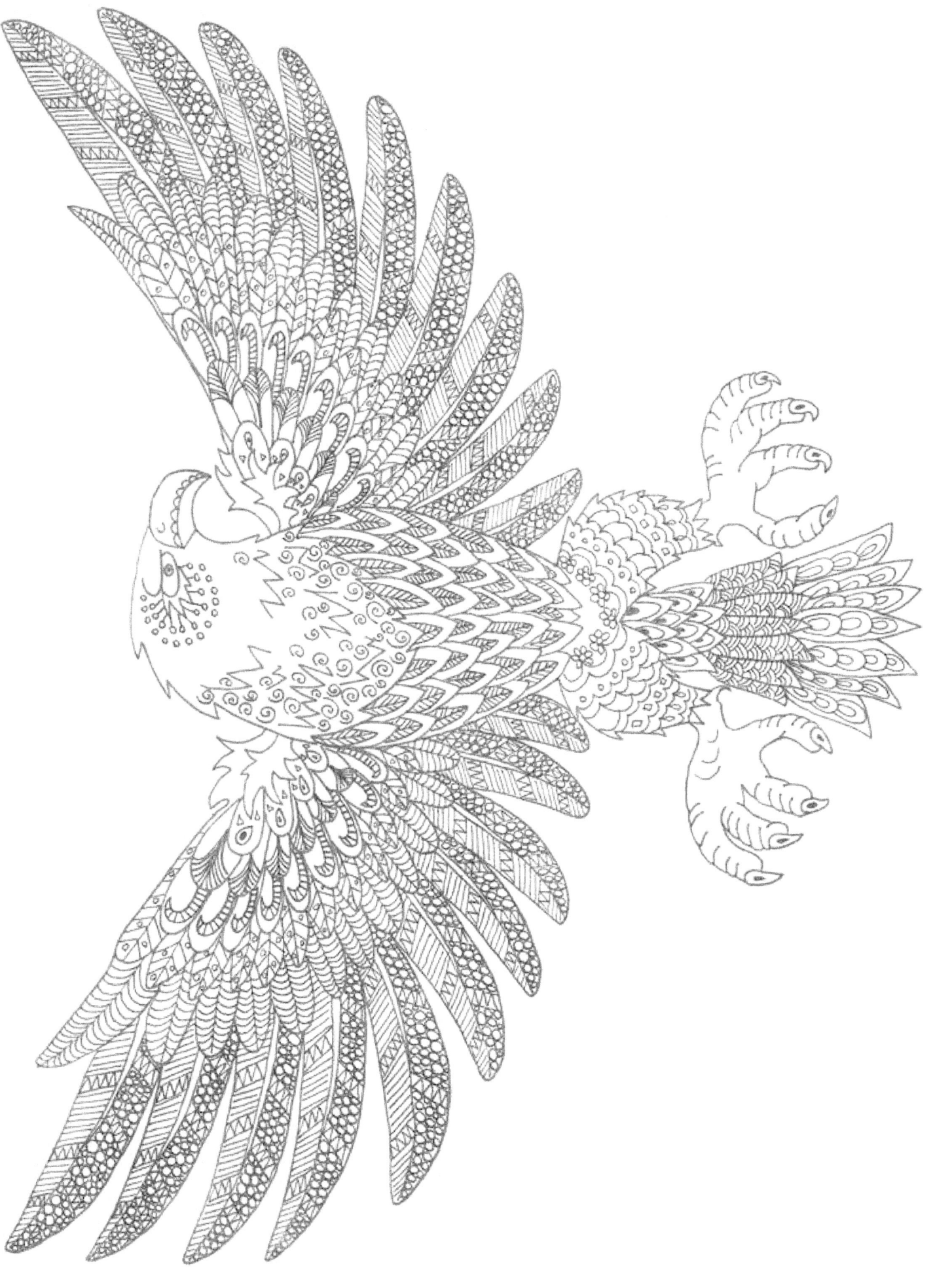

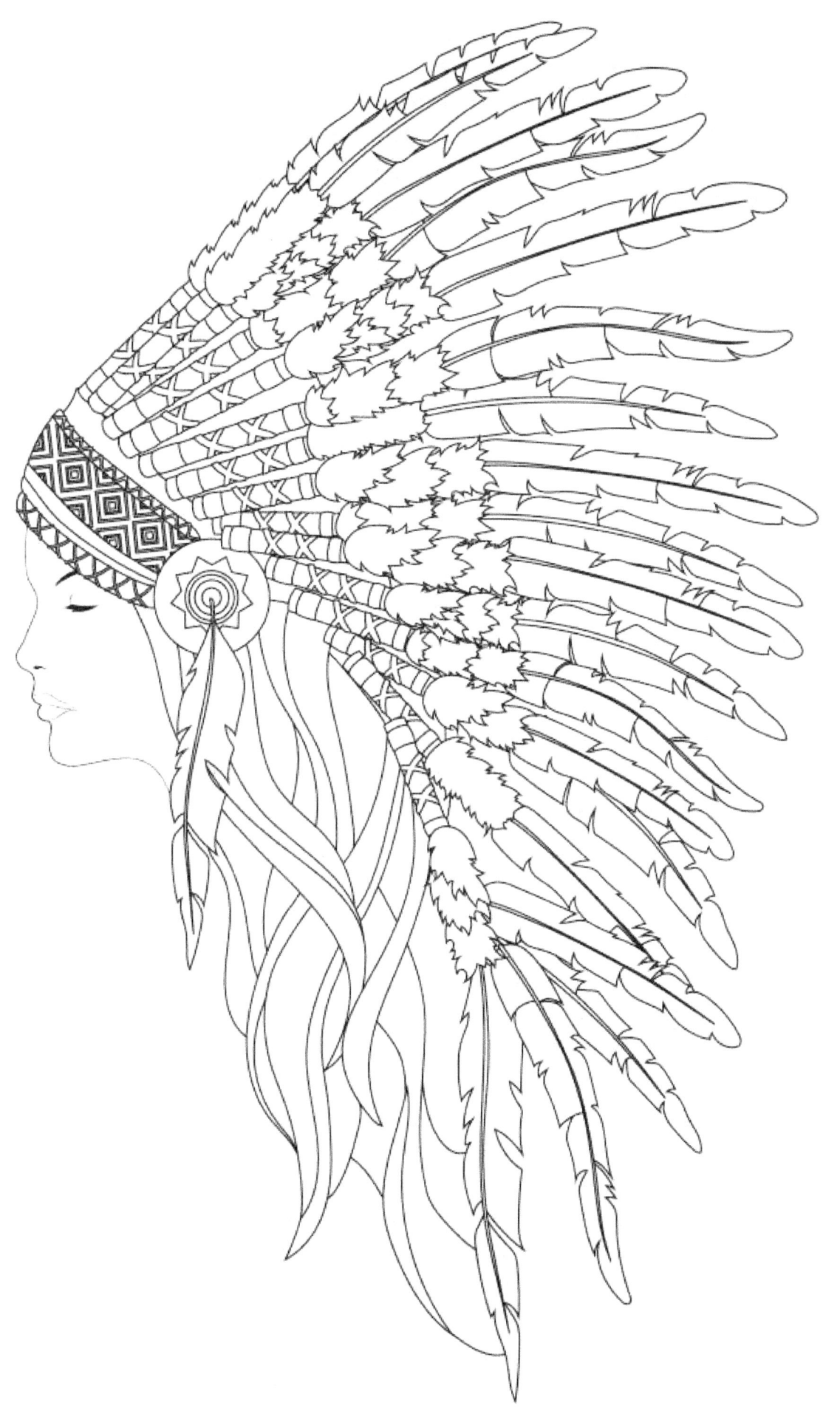

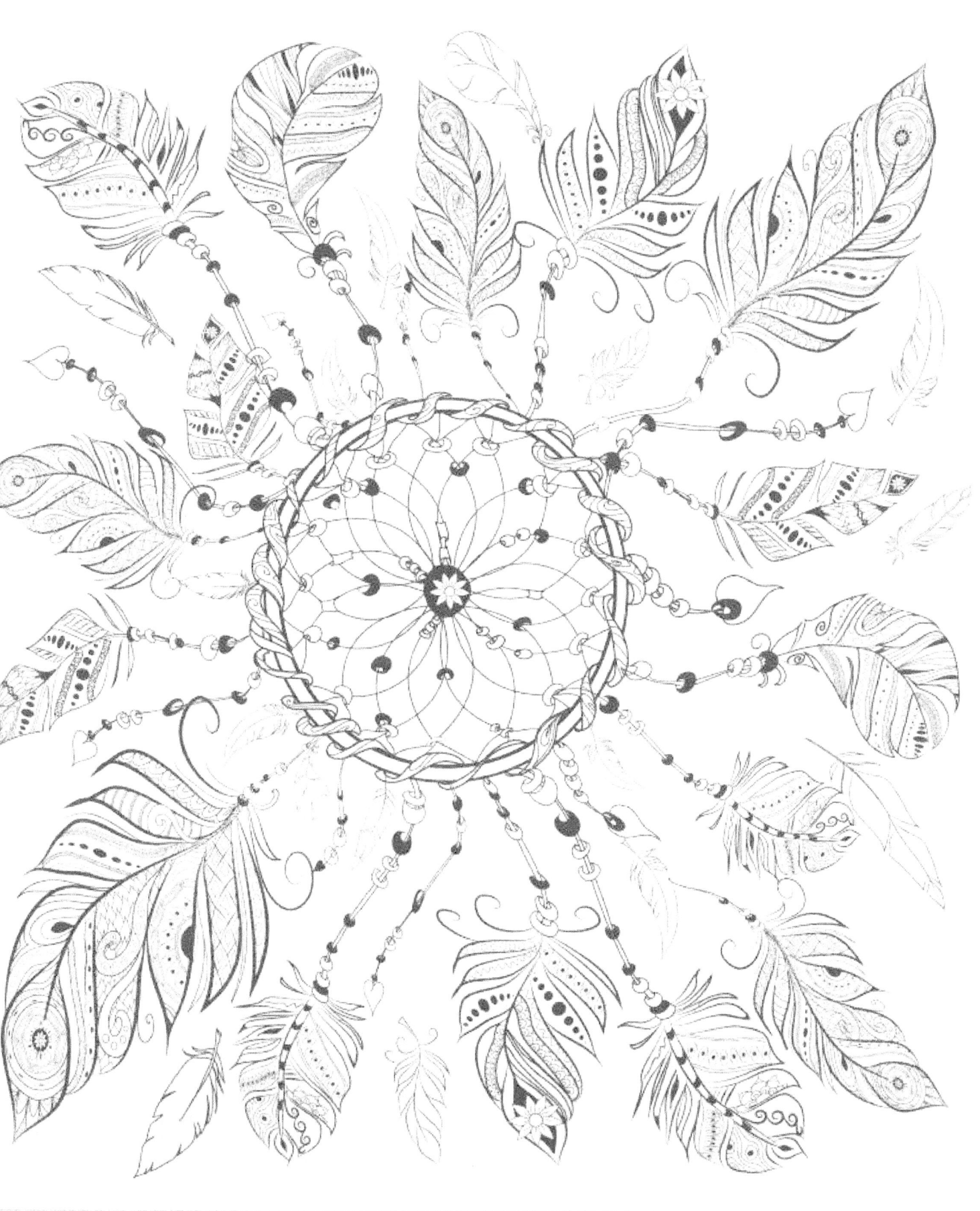

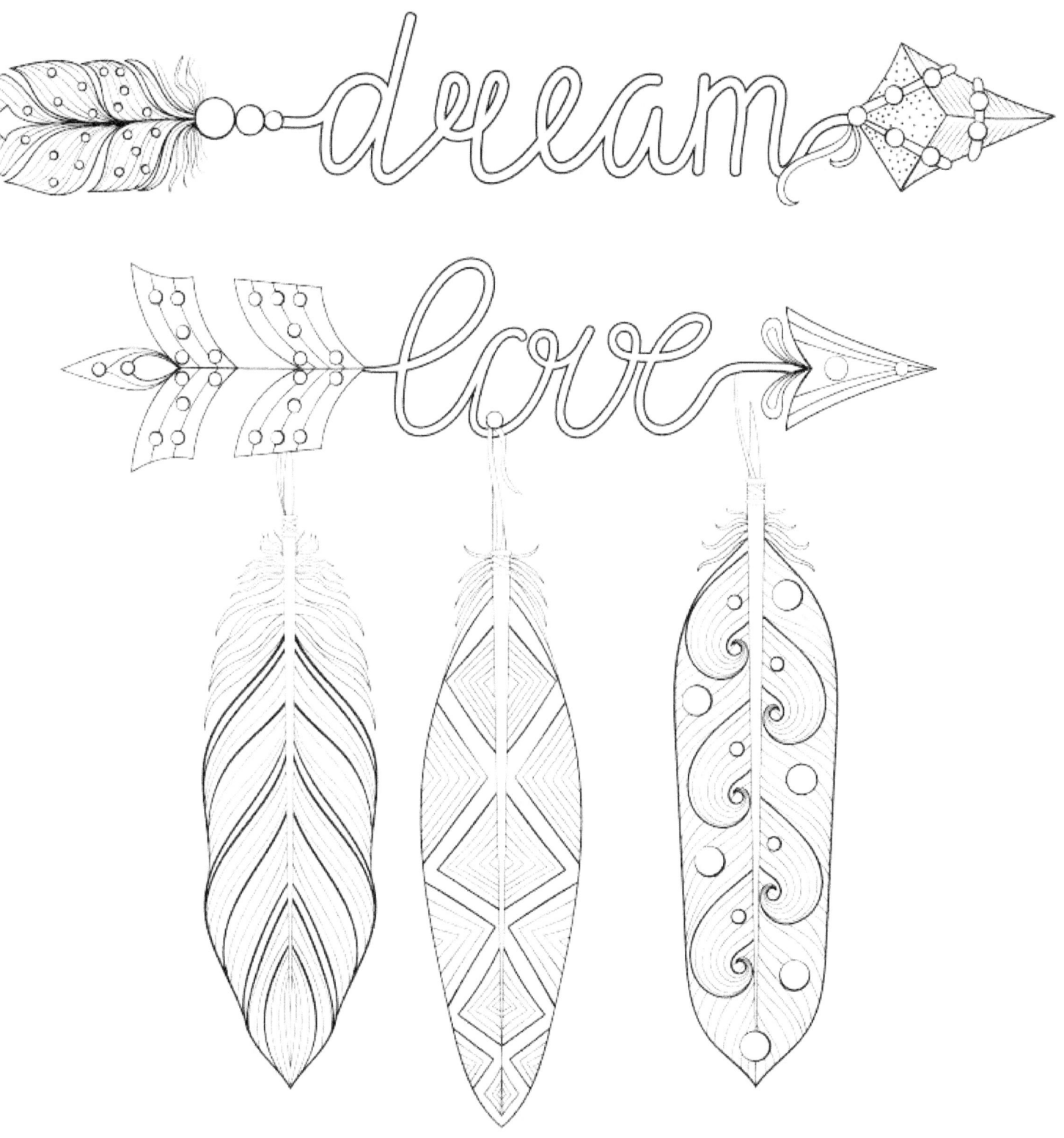

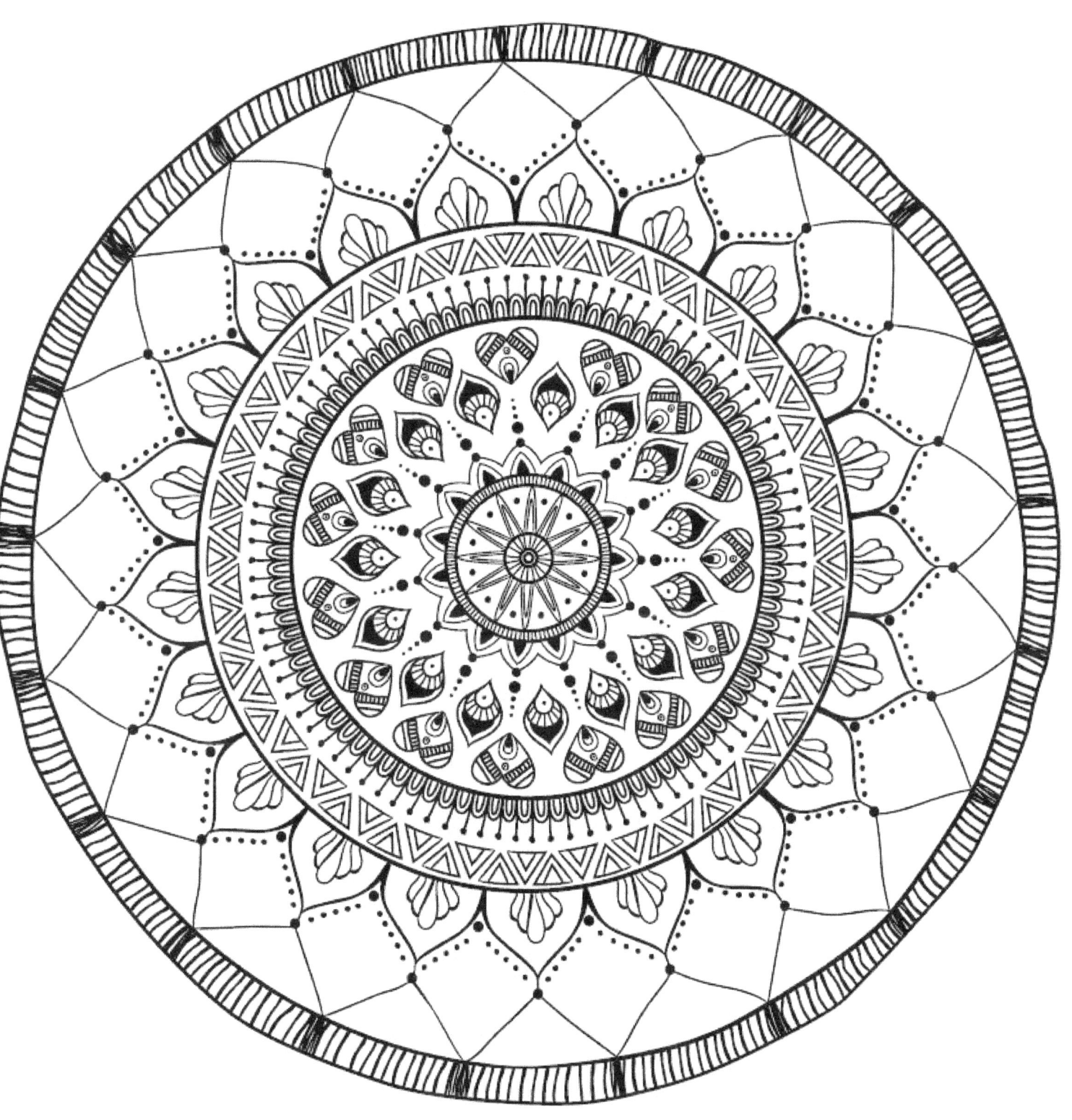

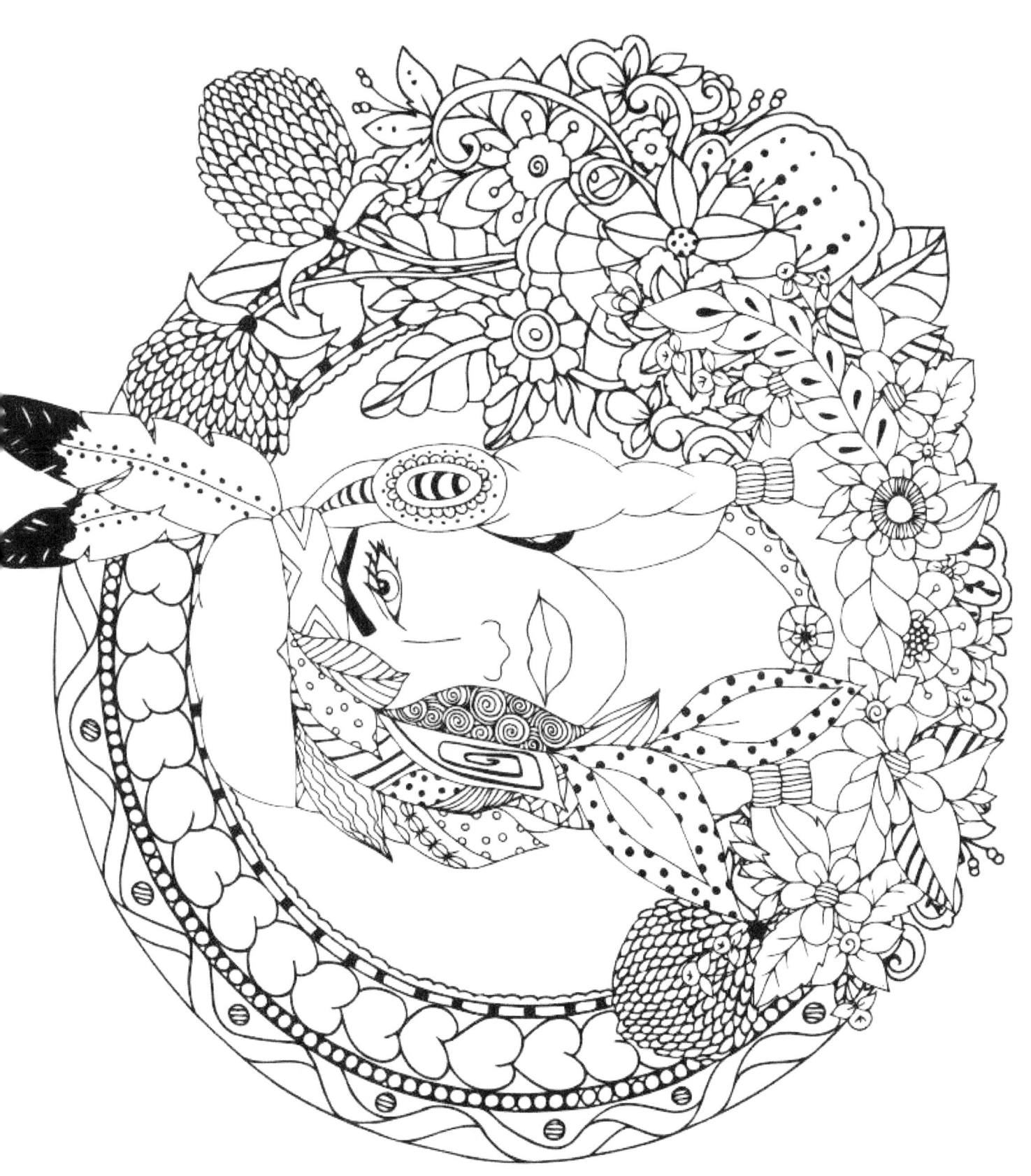

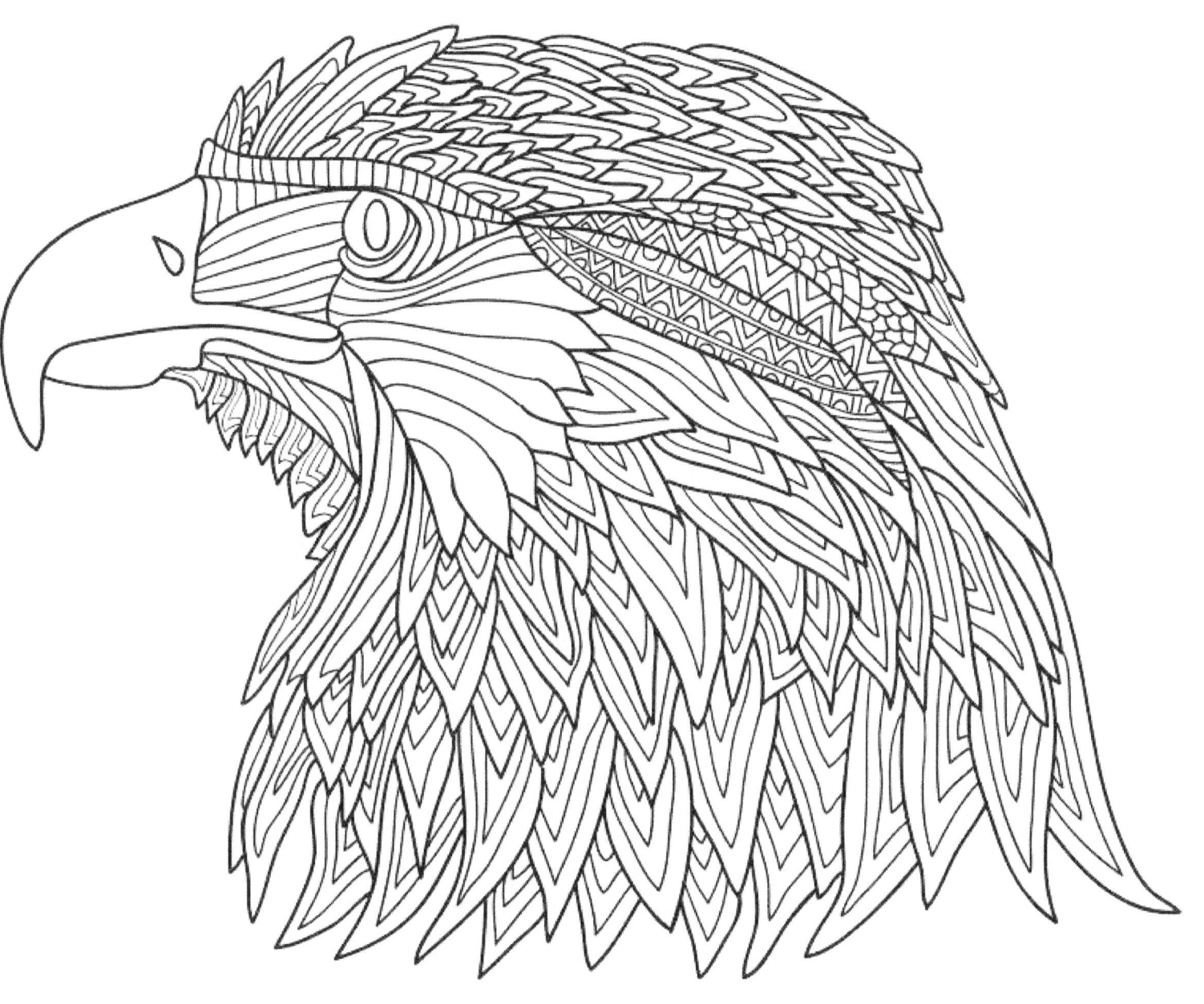

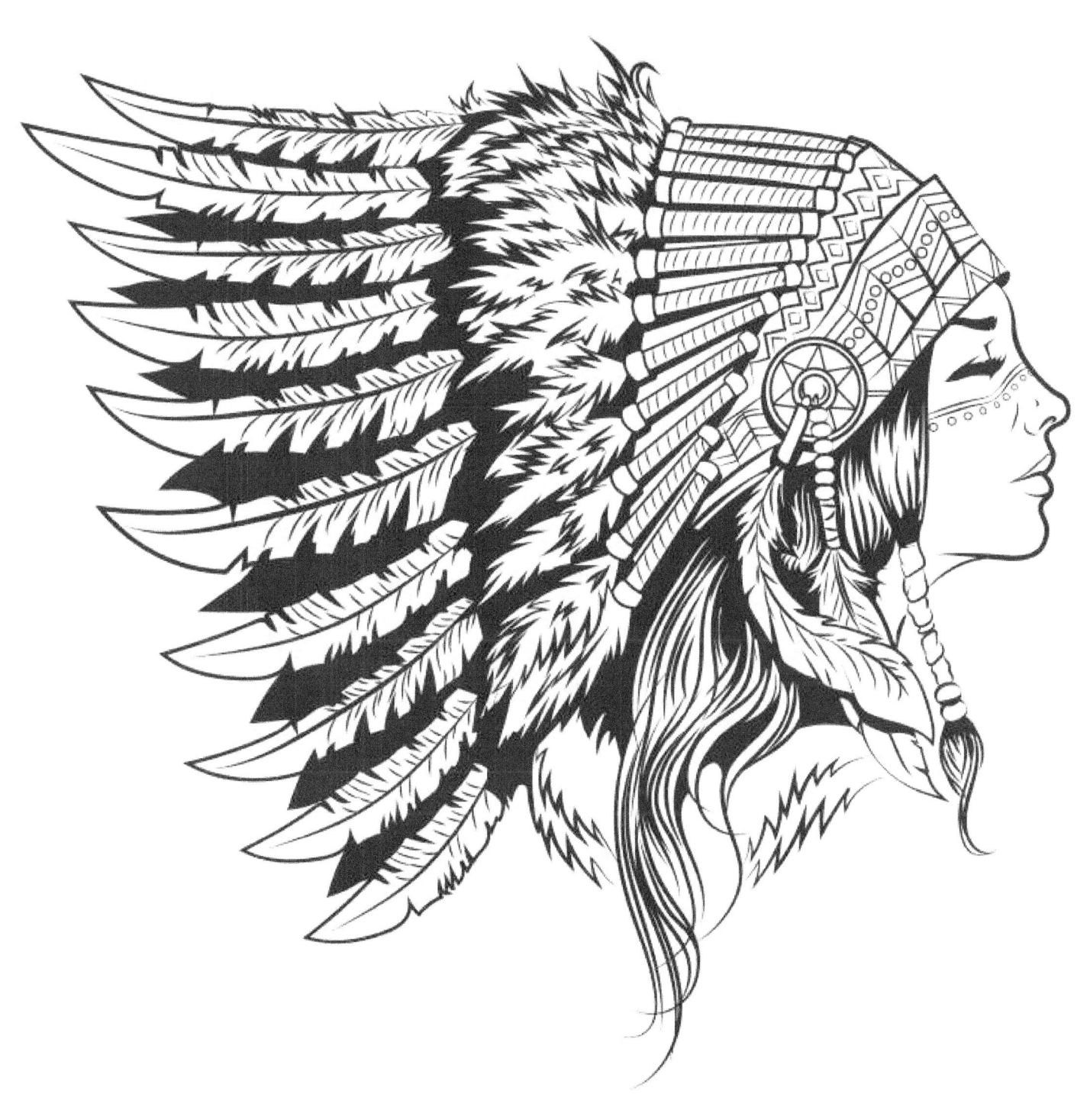

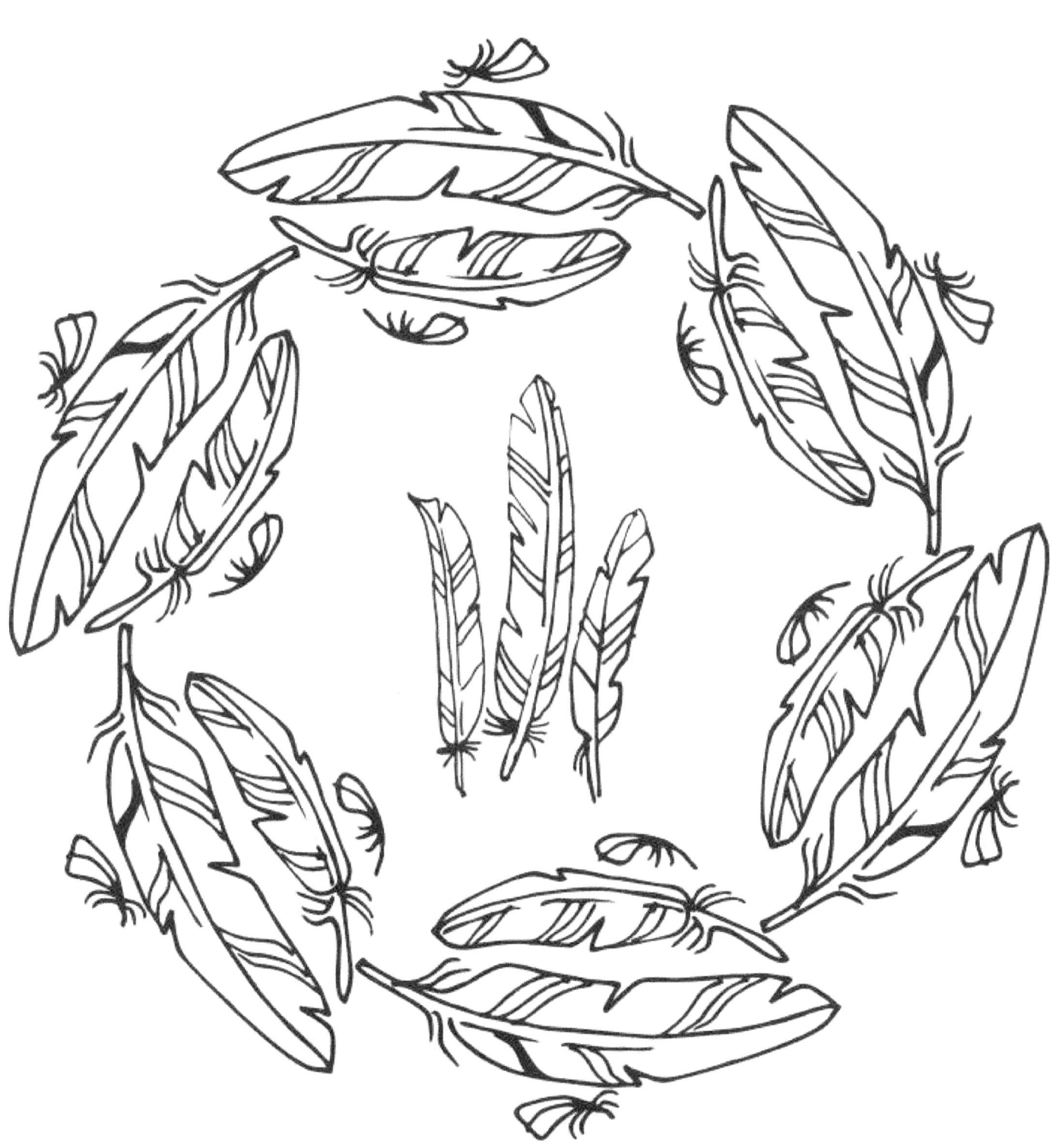

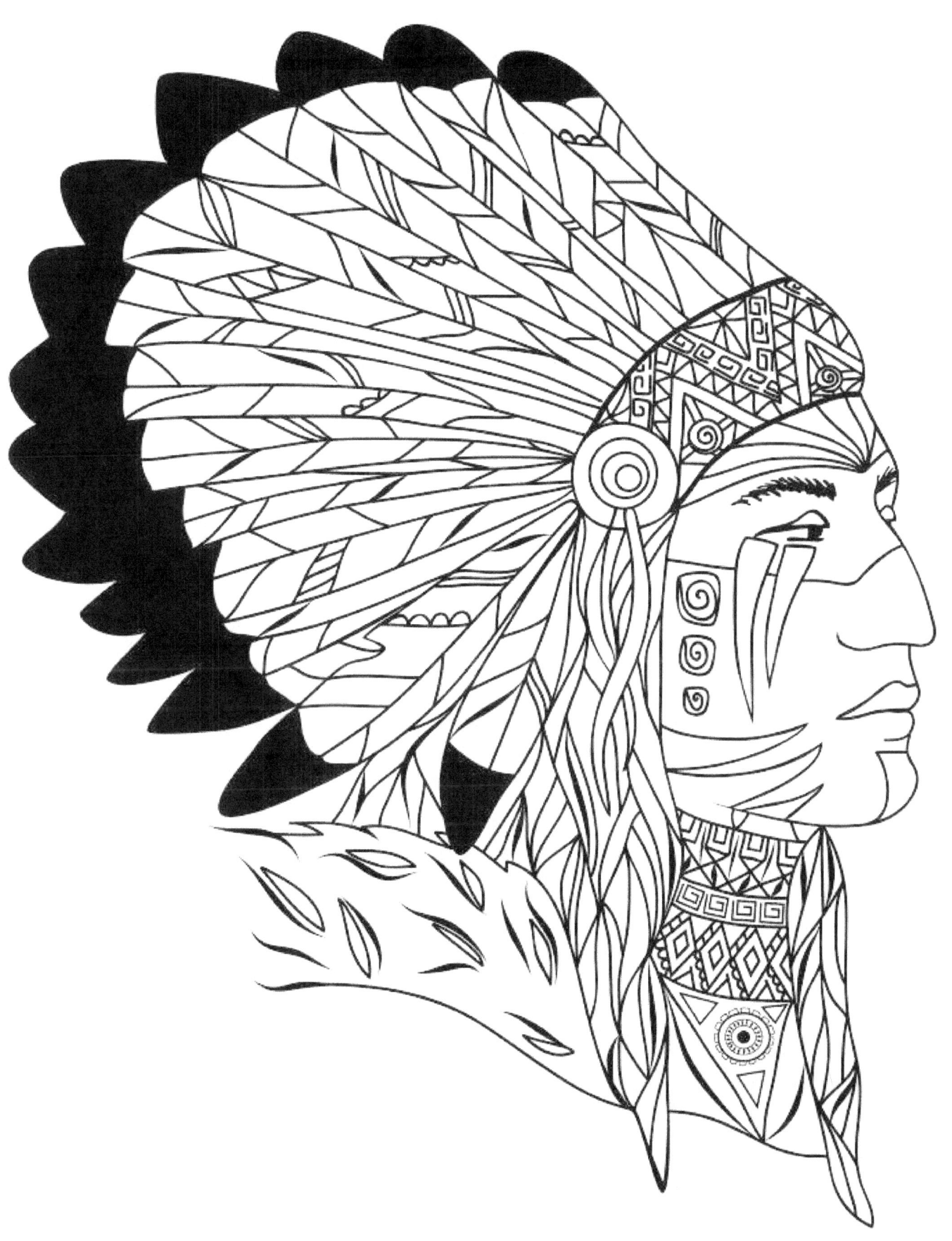

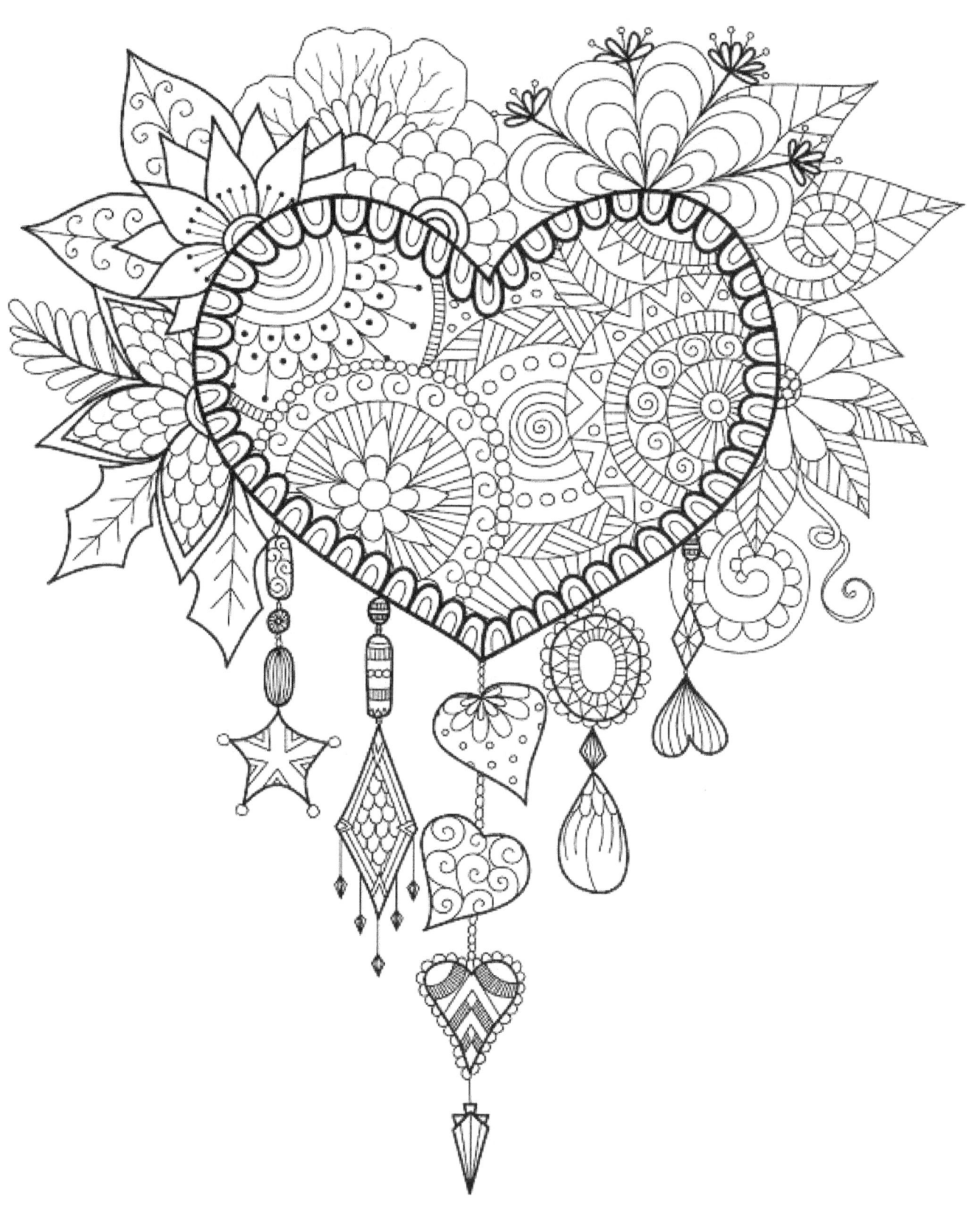

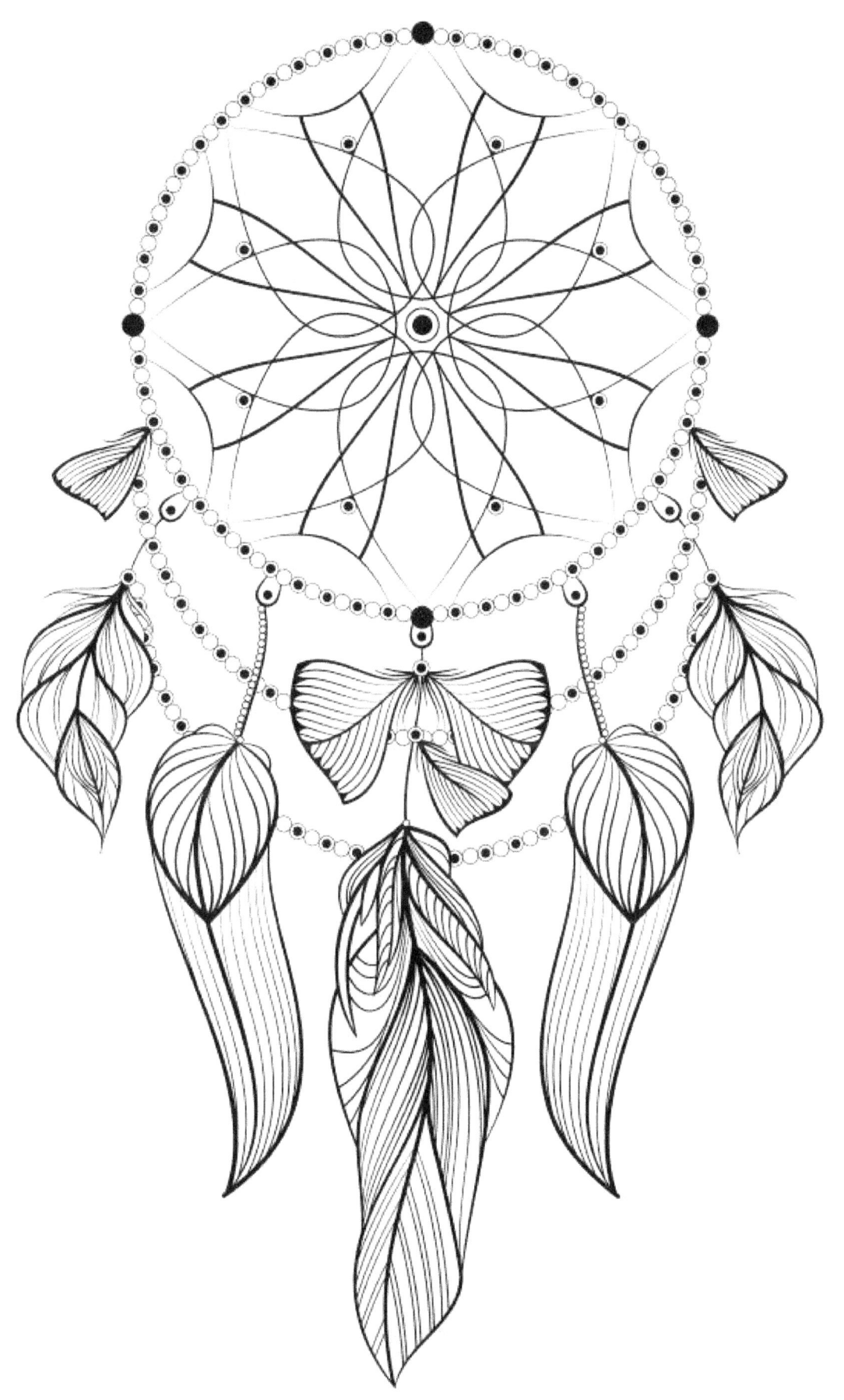

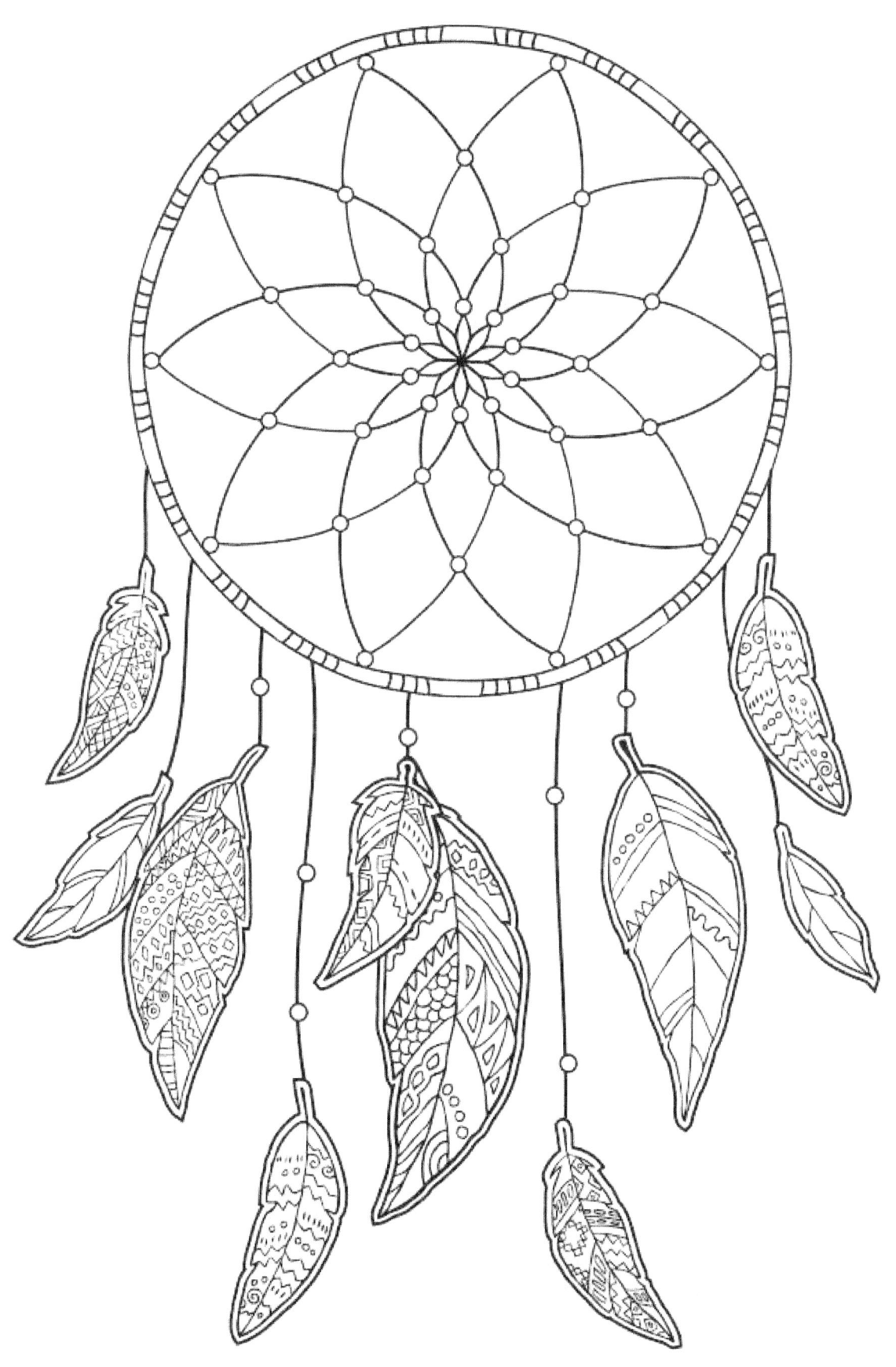

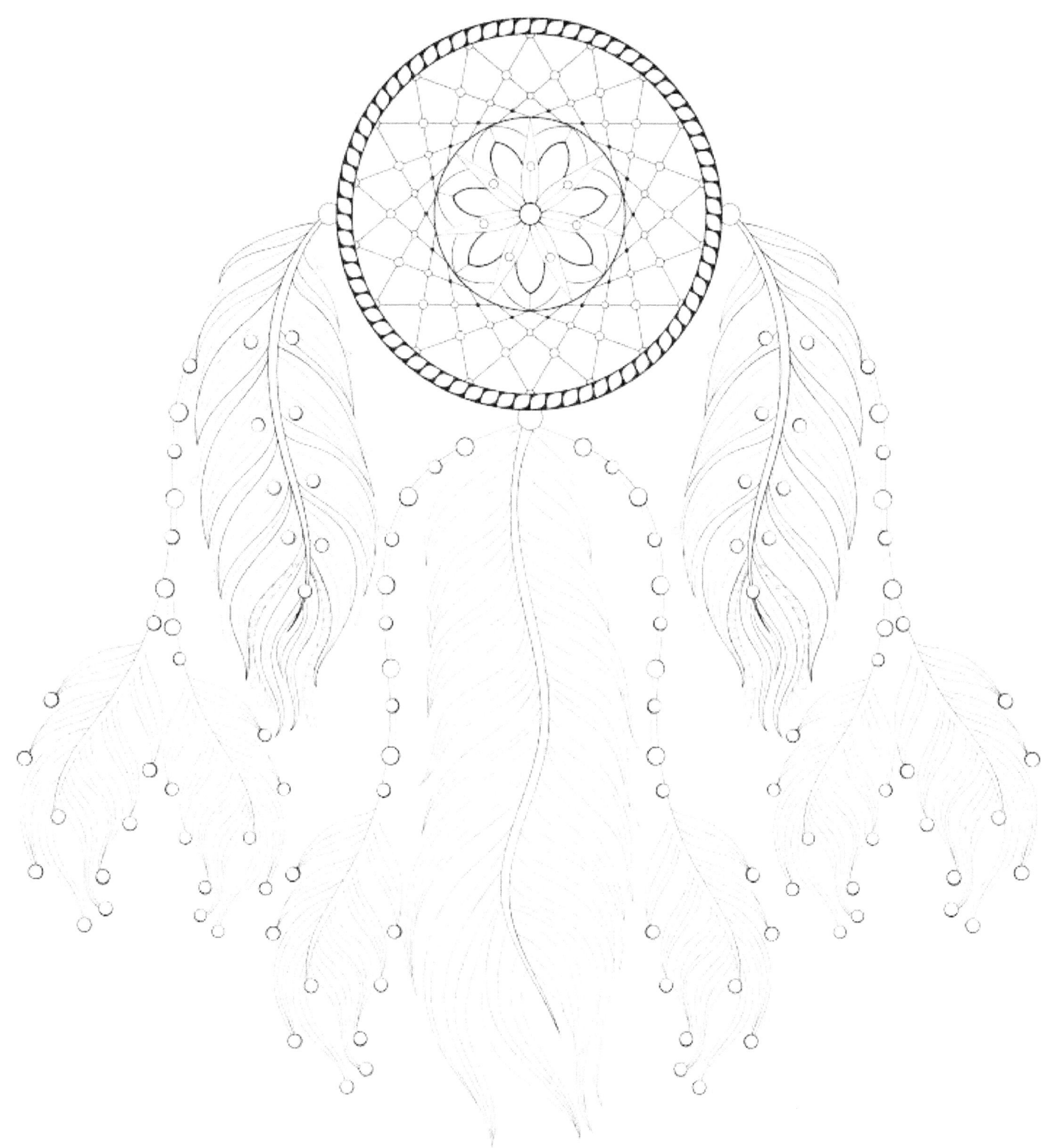

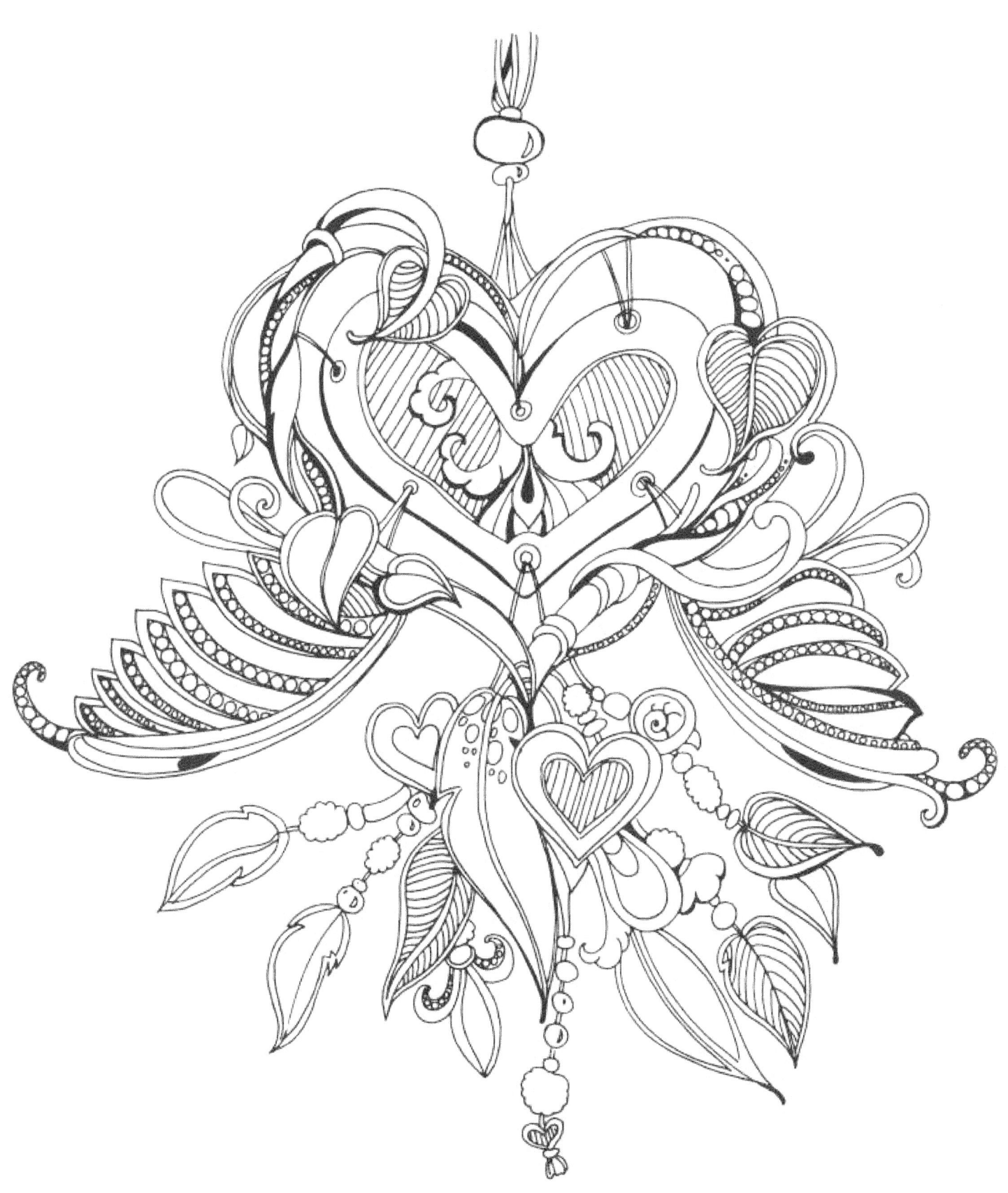

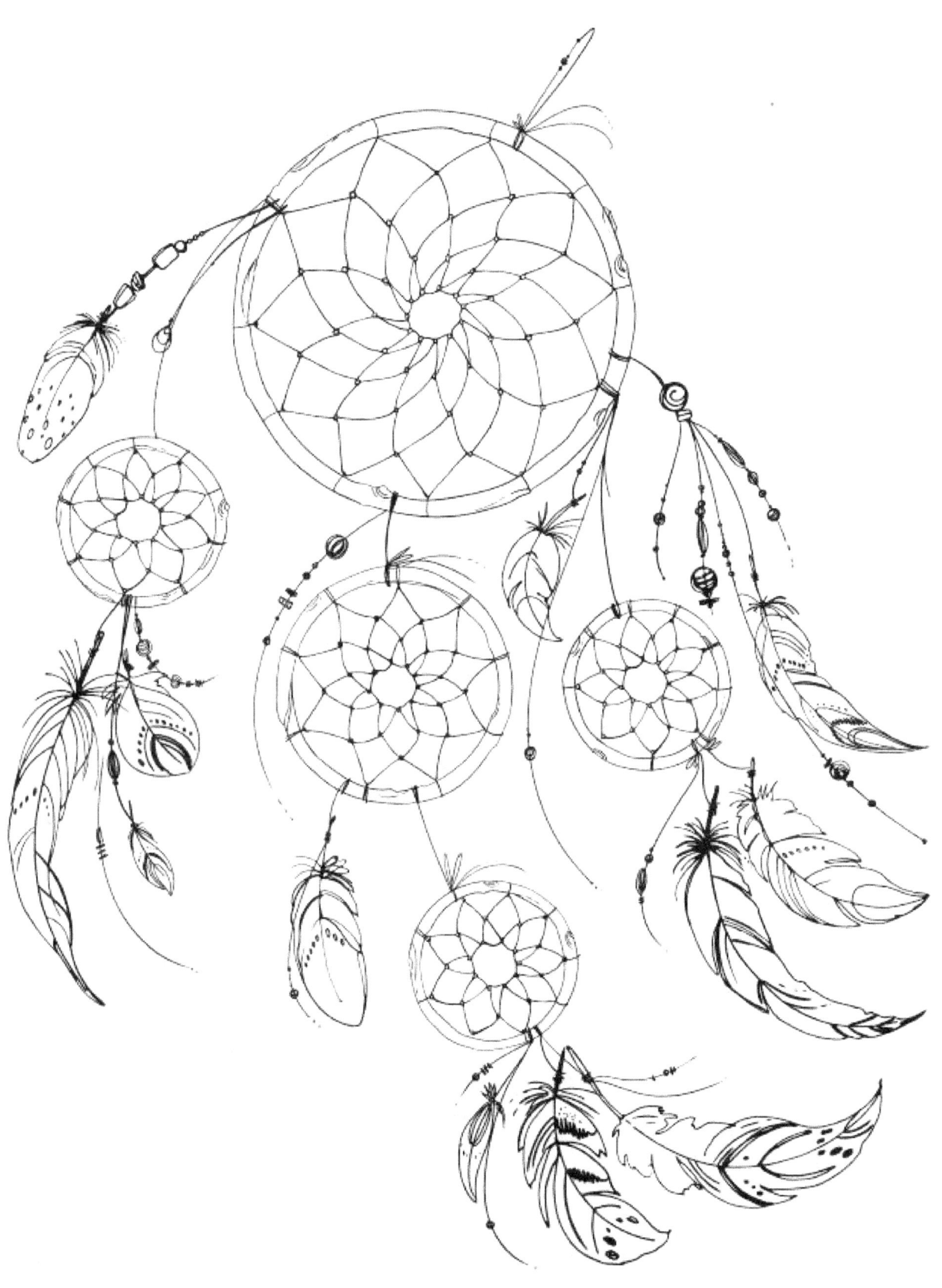

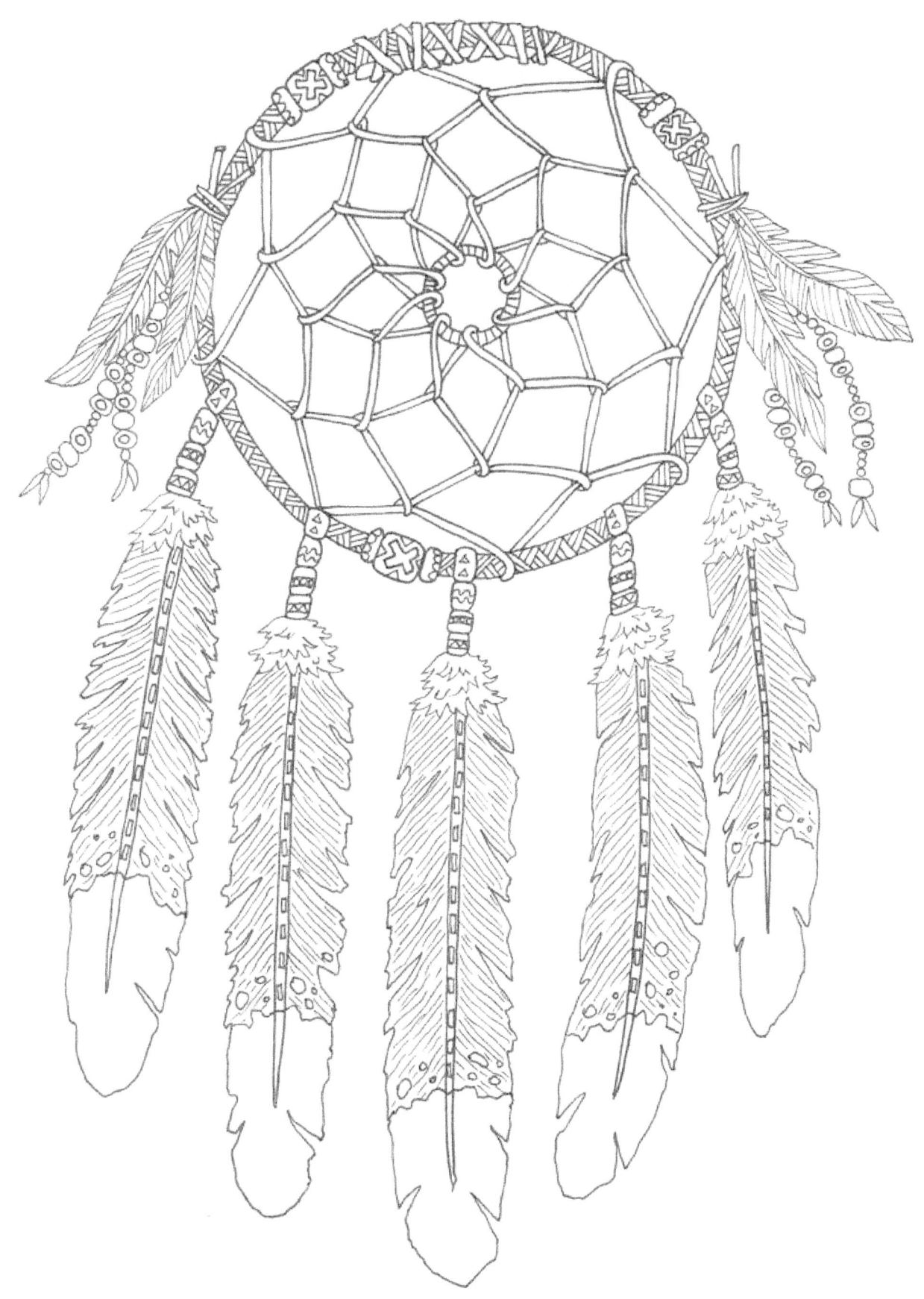

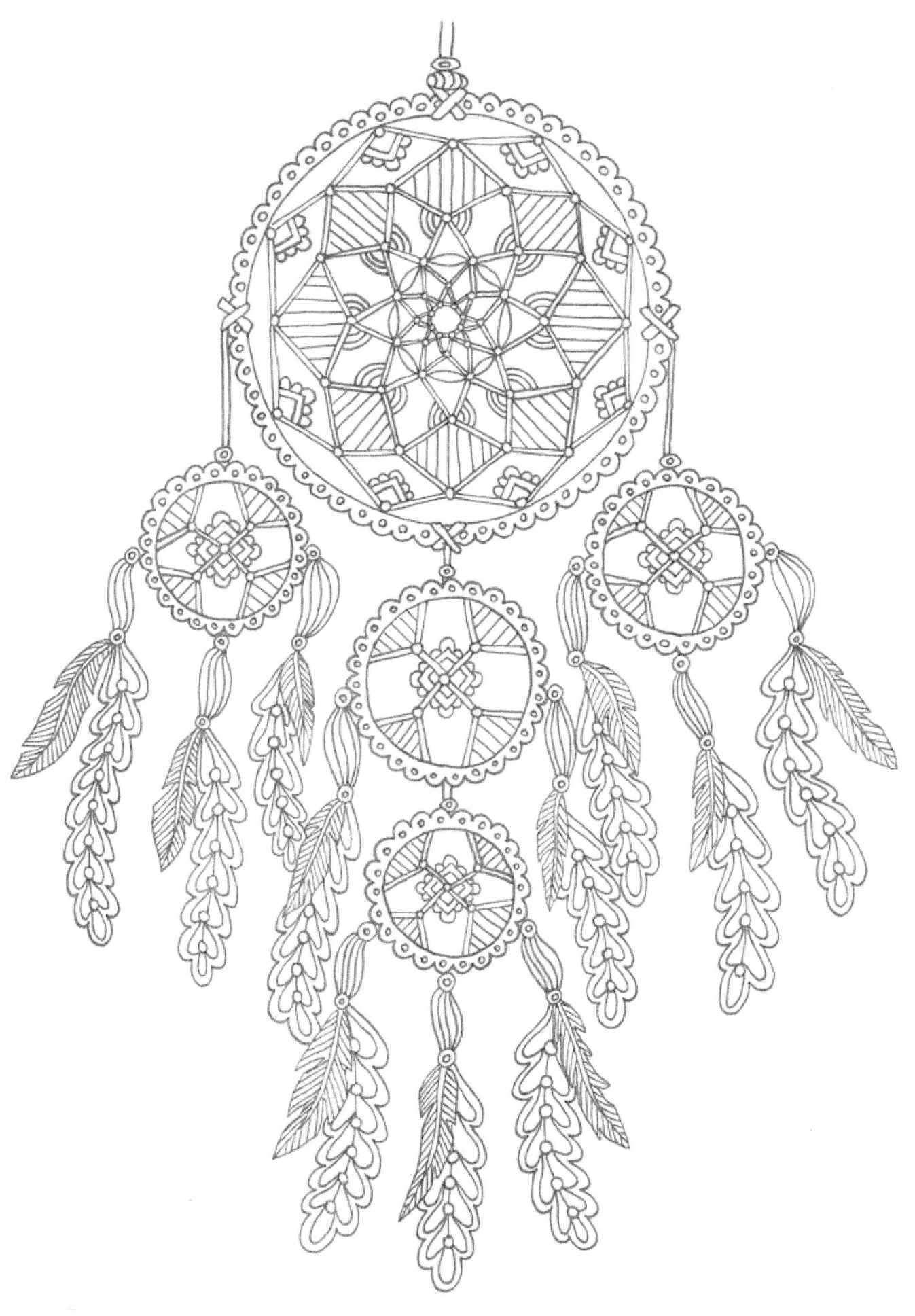

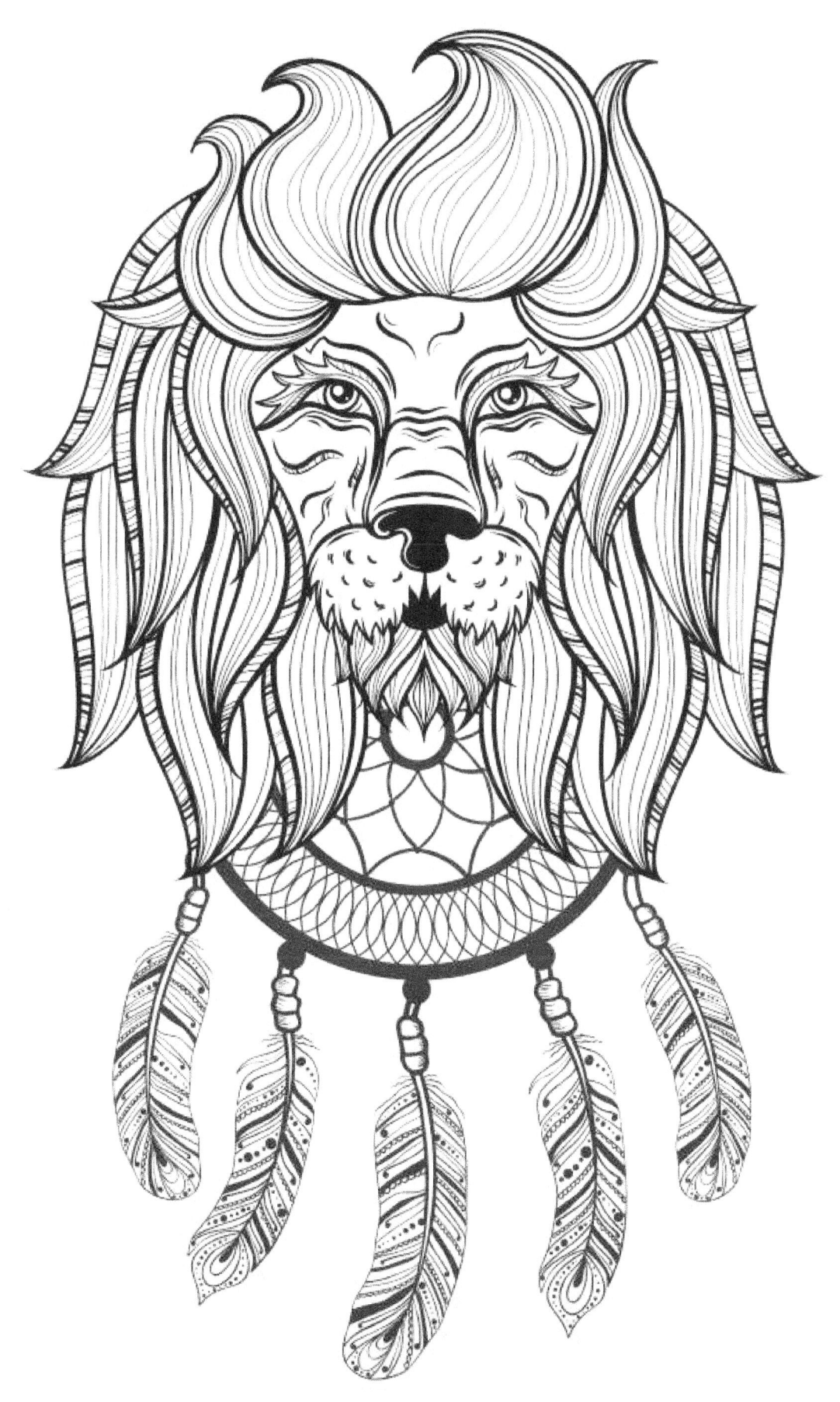

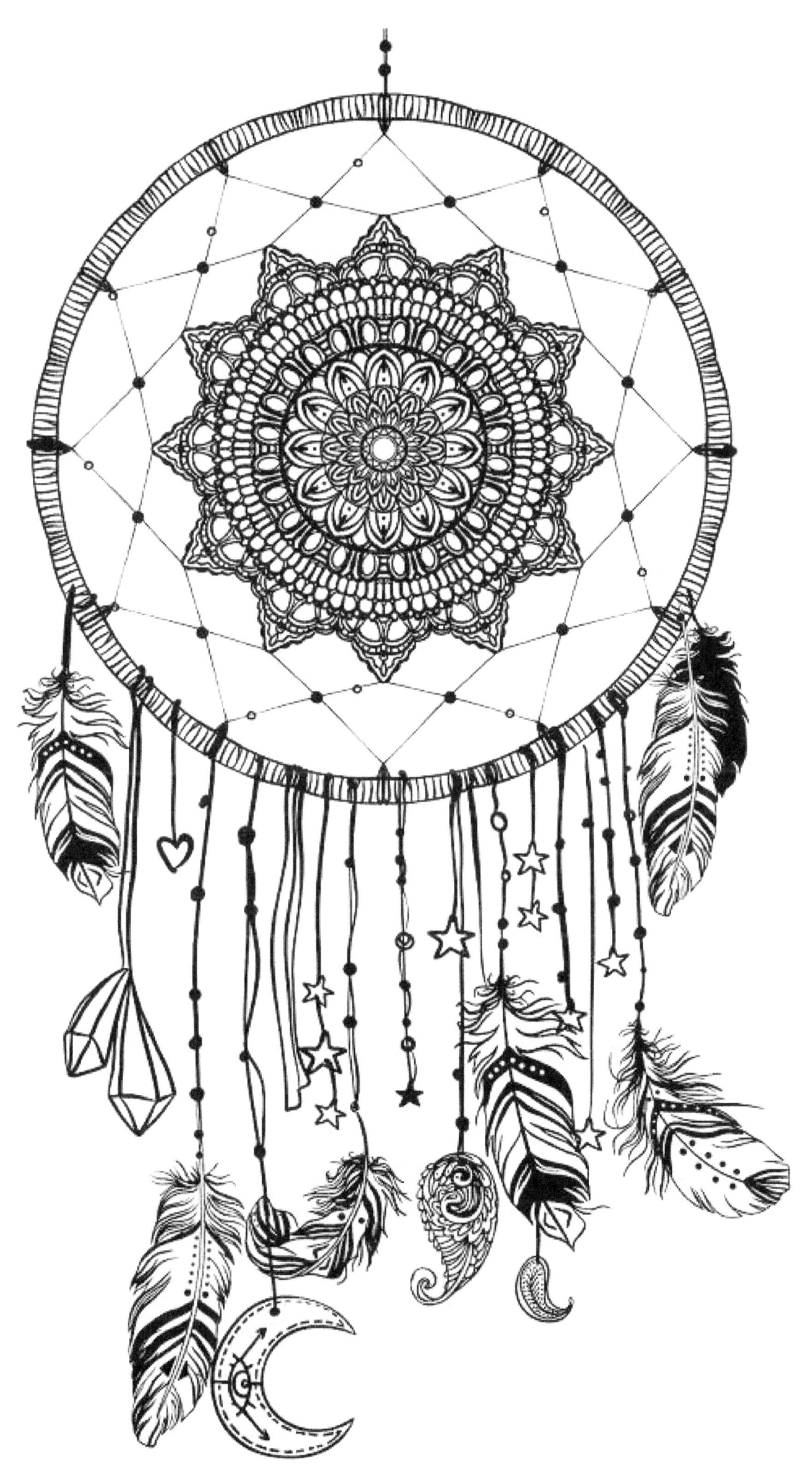

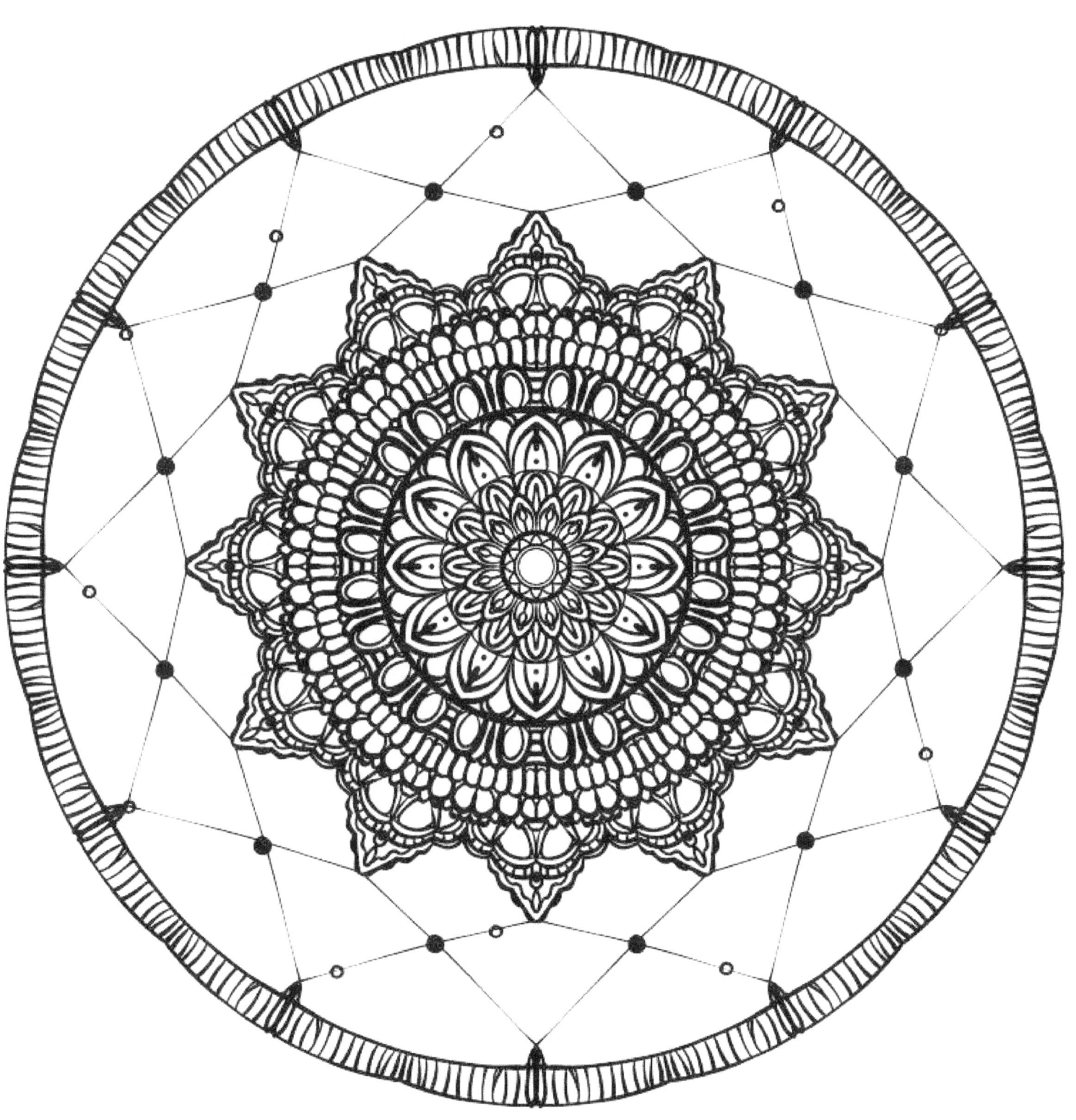

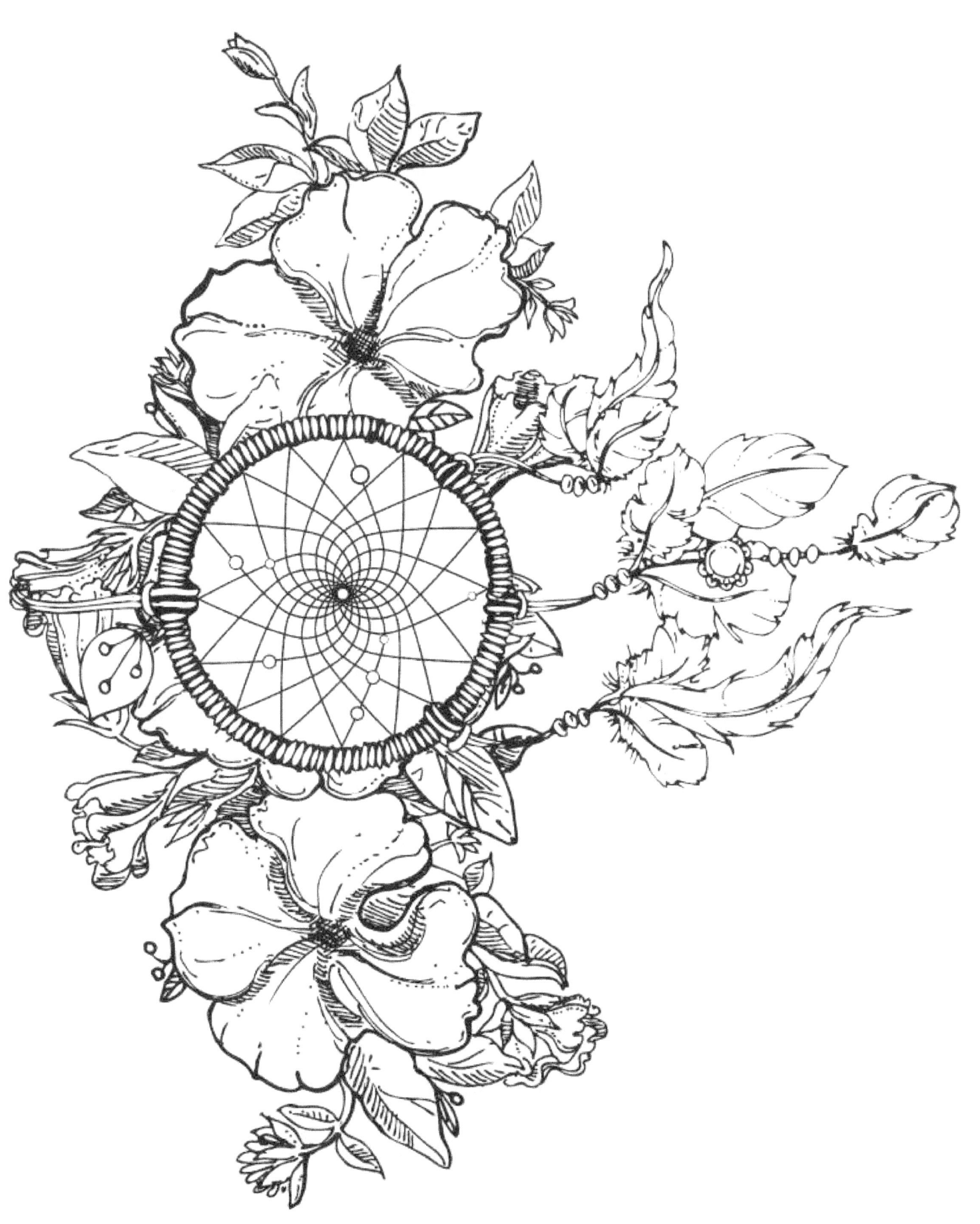

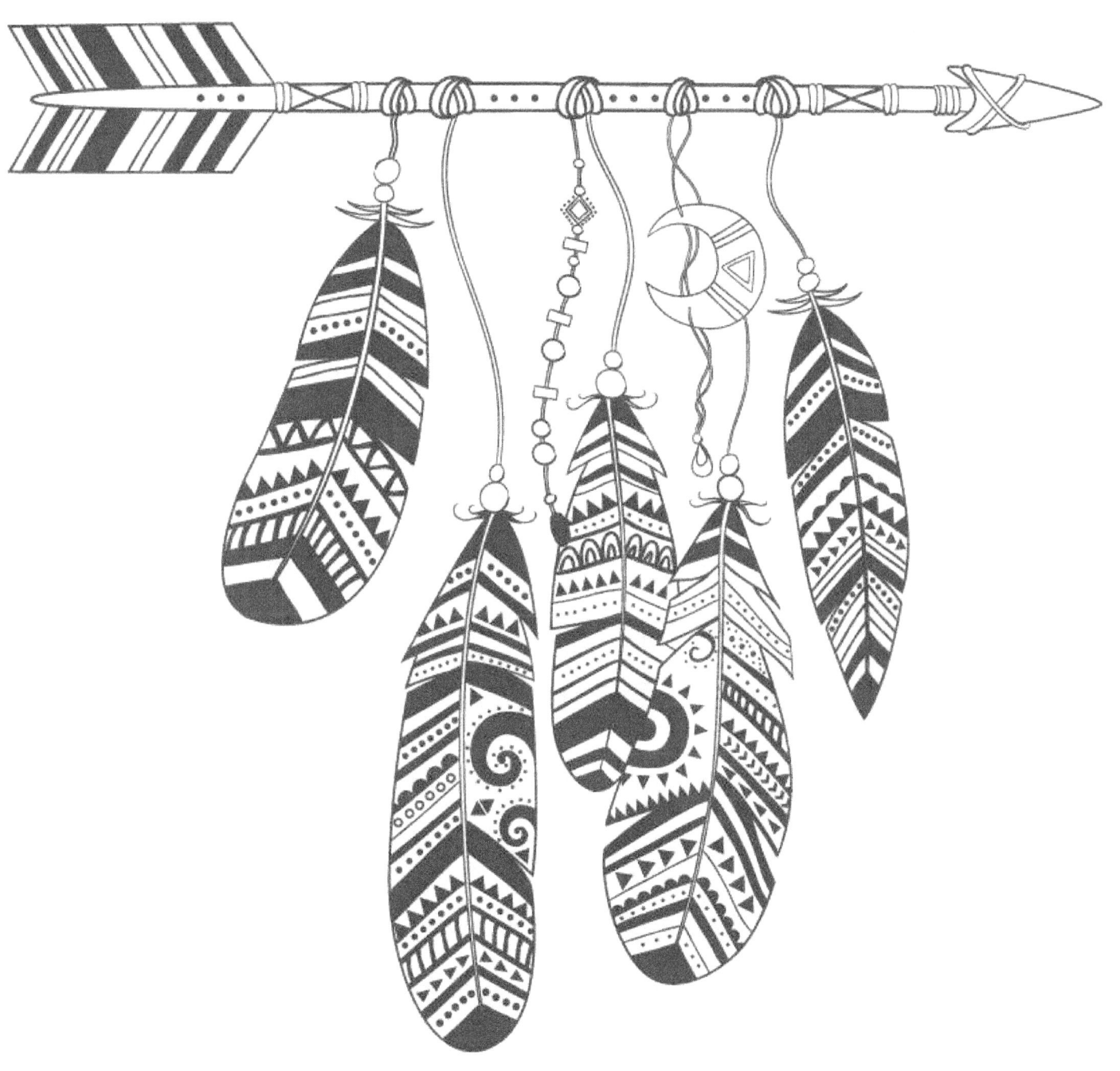

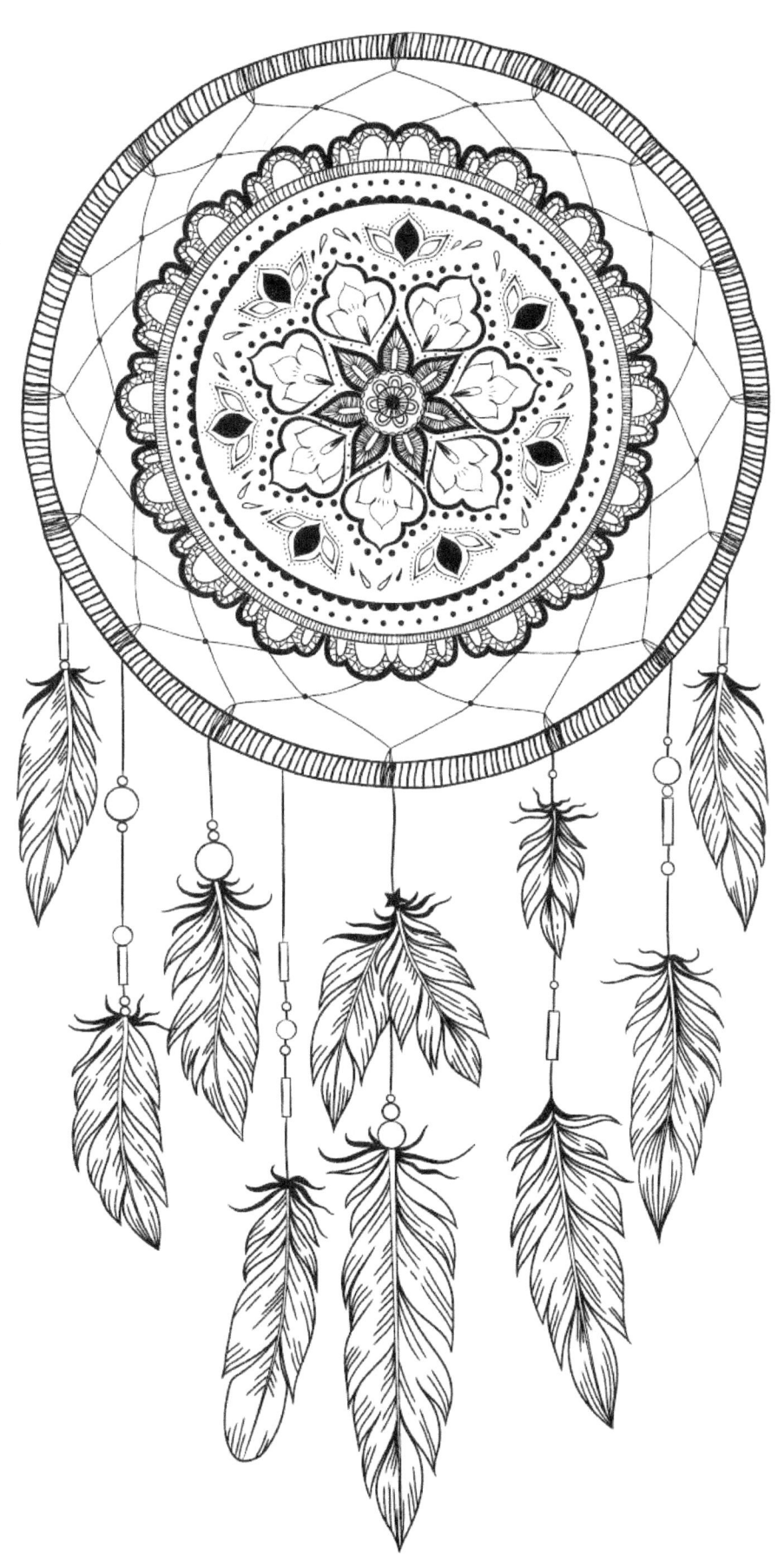

Free Surprise Bonus! We know how much native Americans loved their horses, so we thought it would be a nice surprise to add these beautiful horse coloring pages. Enjoy!

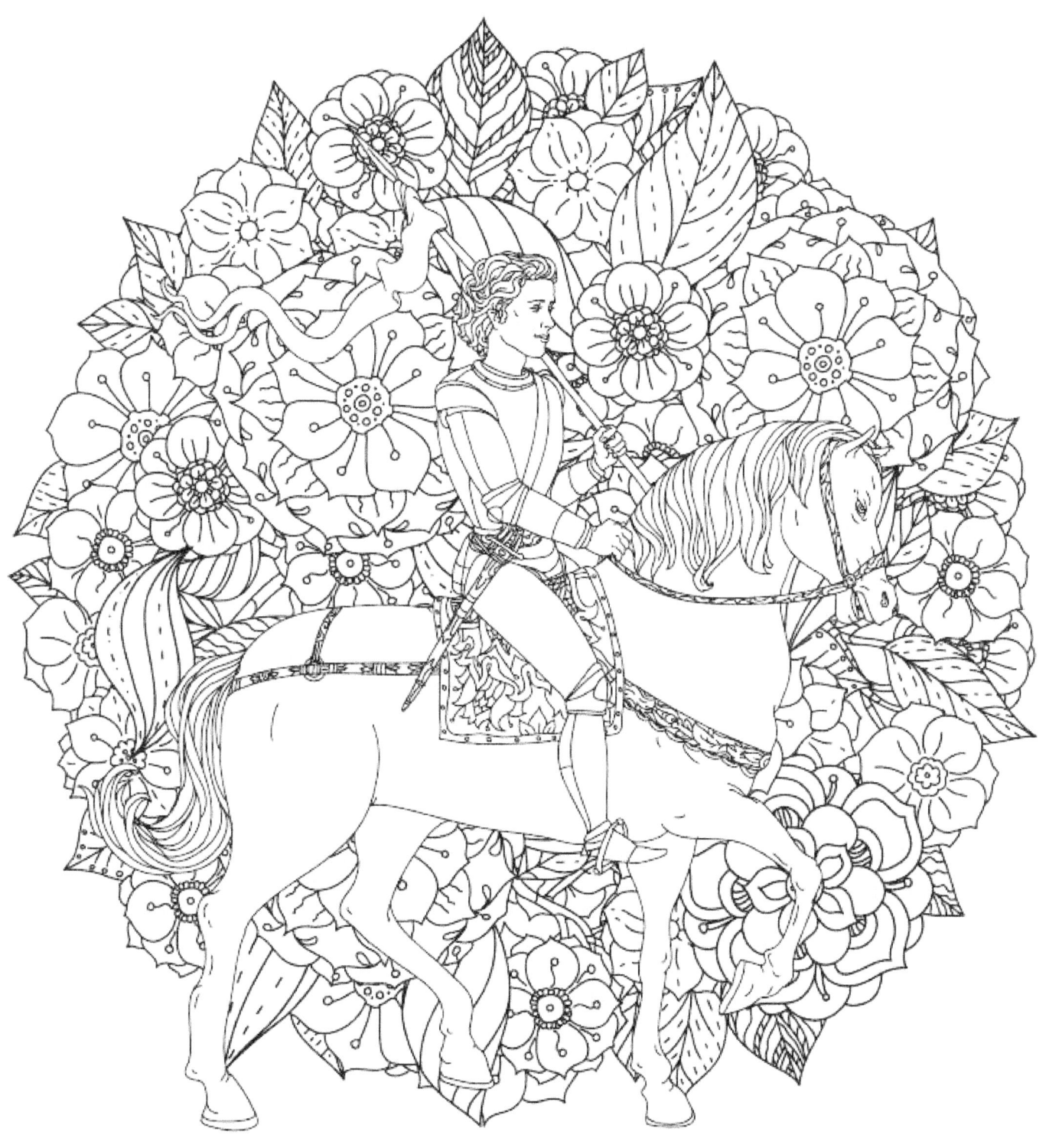

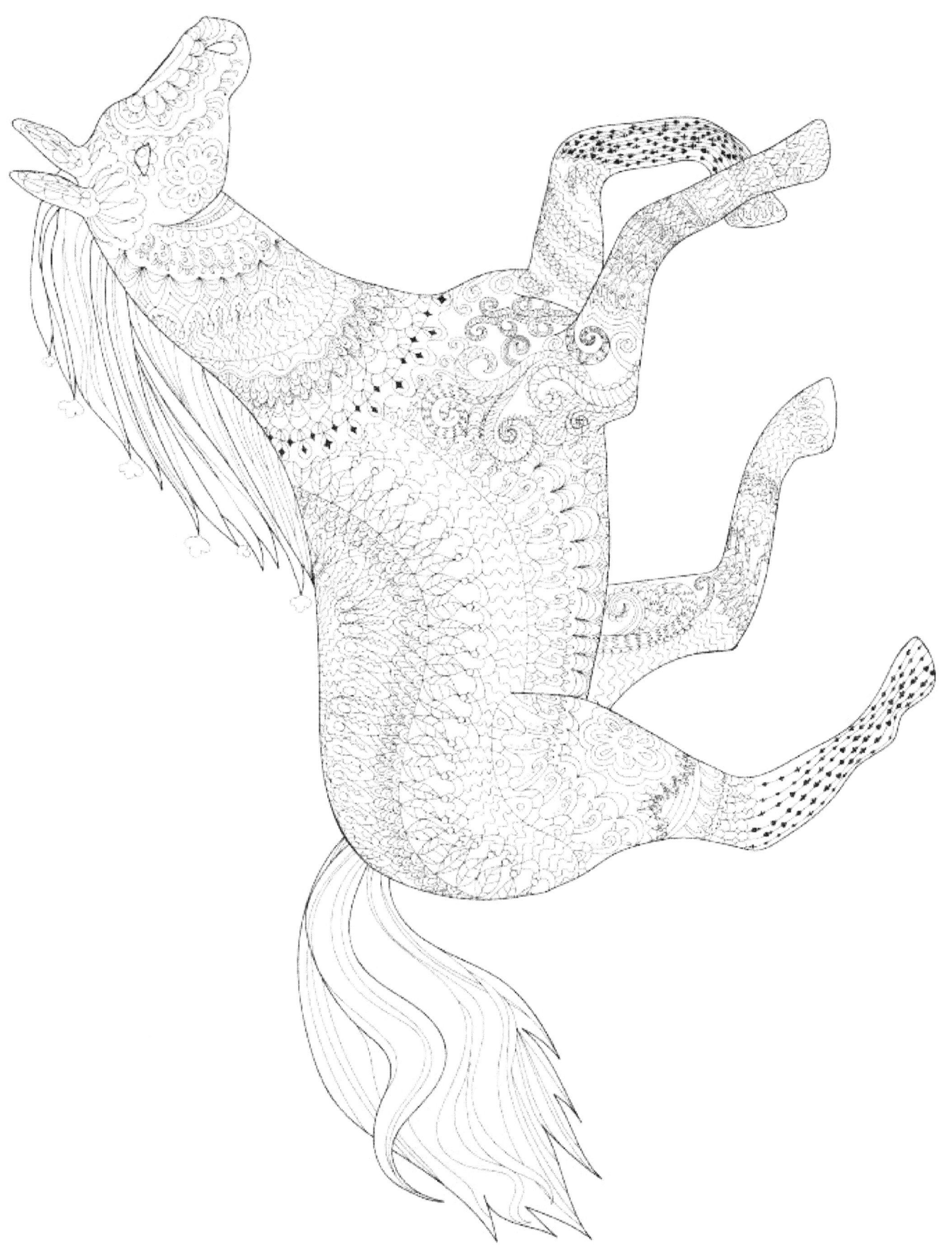

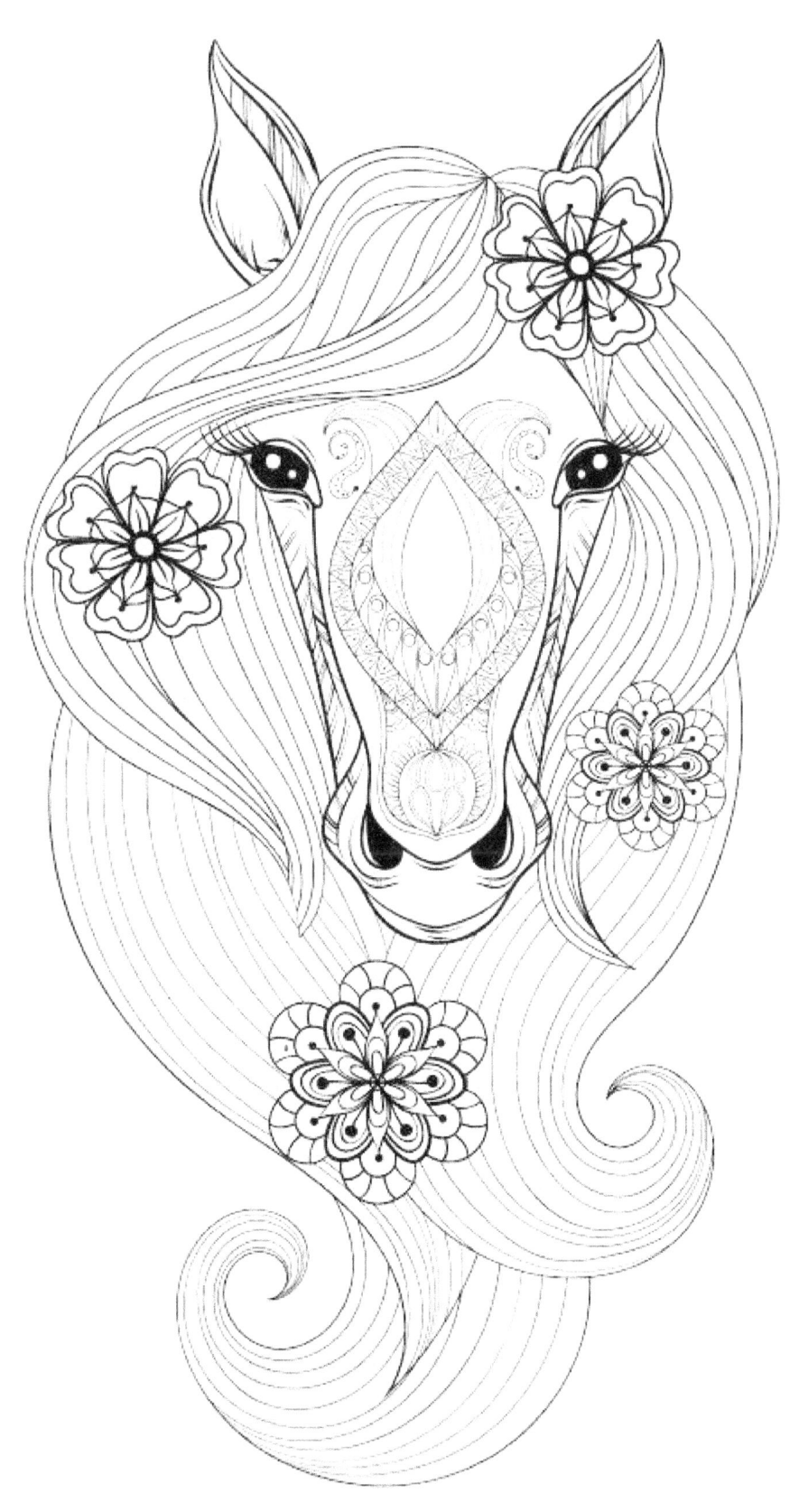

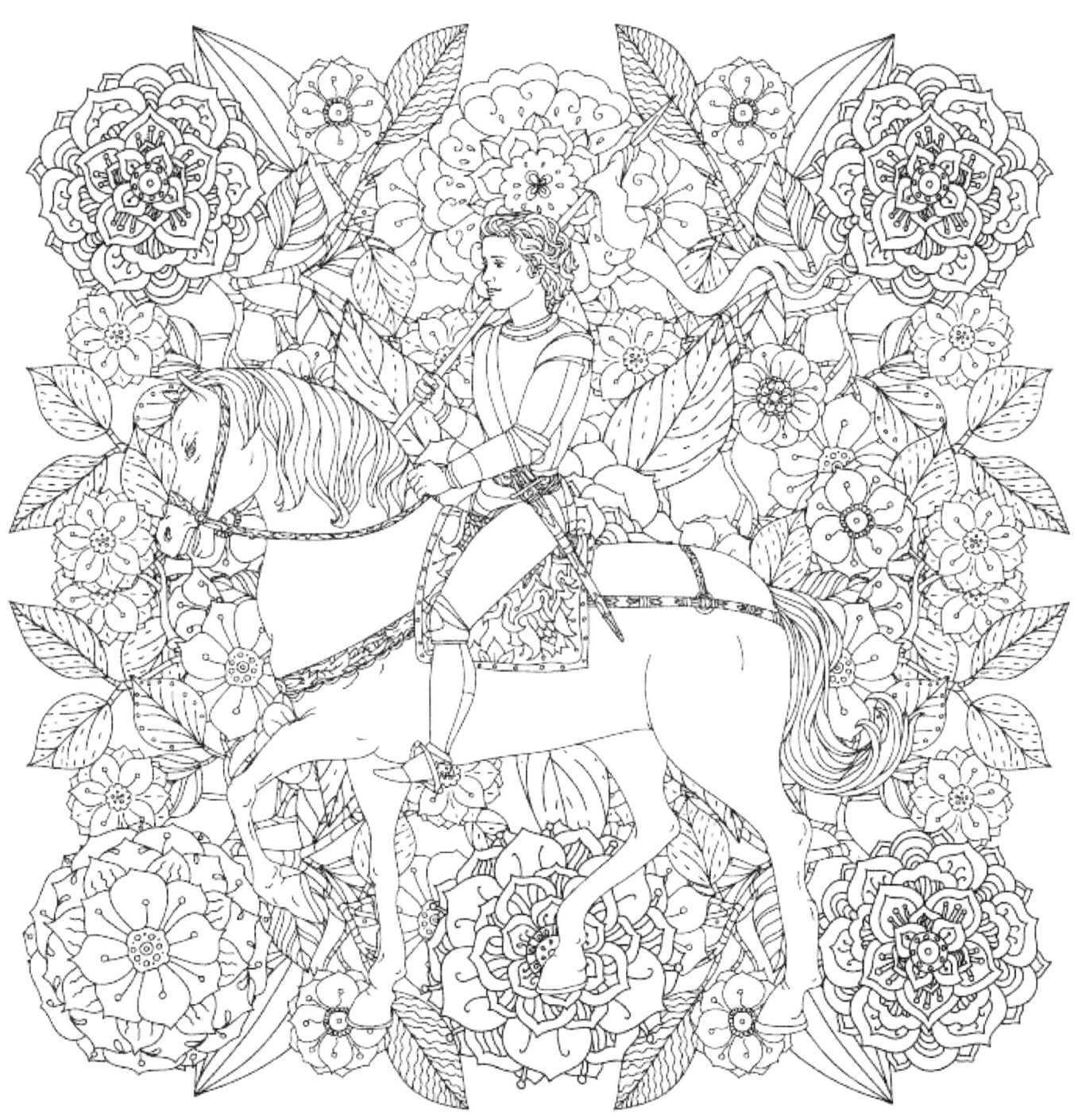

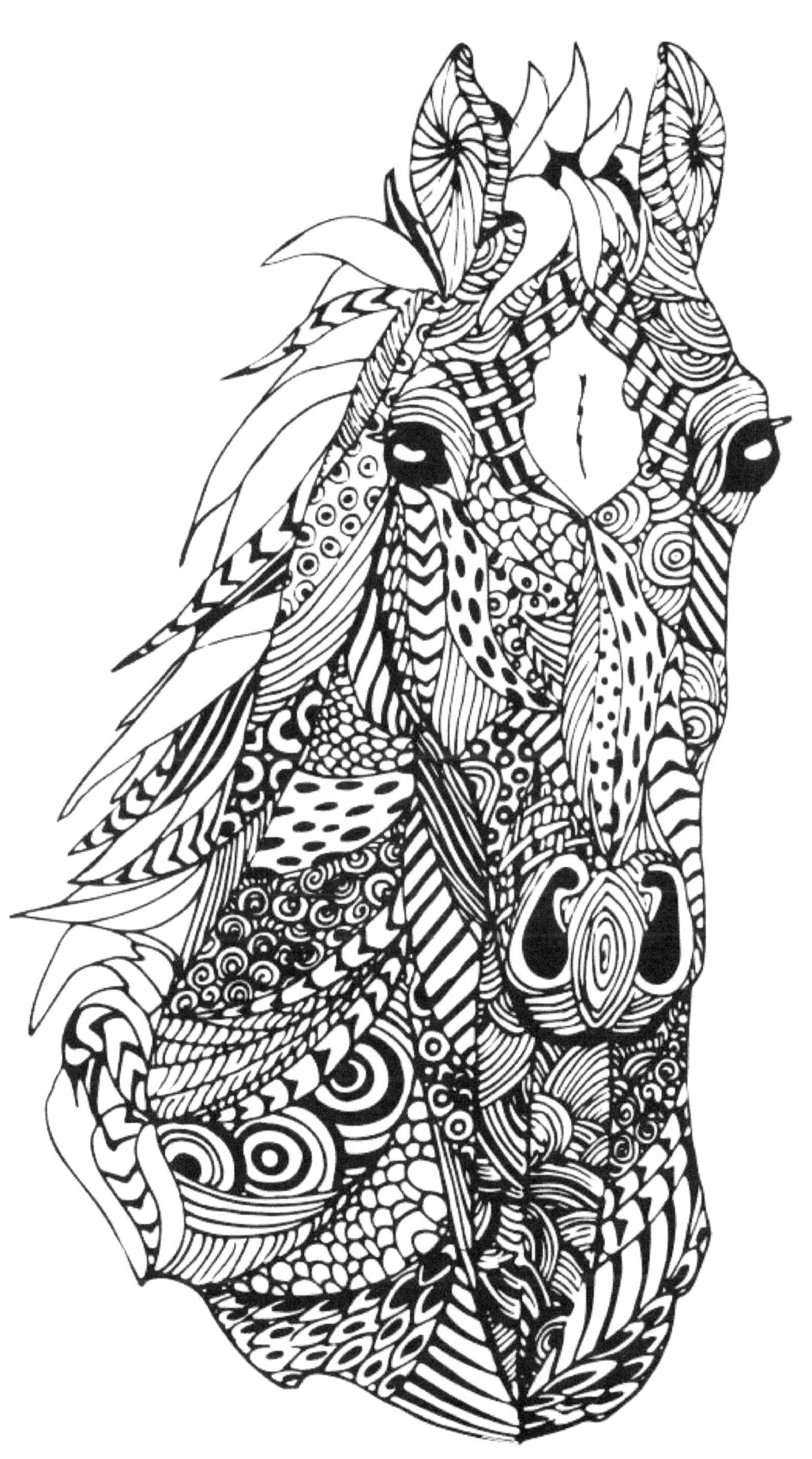

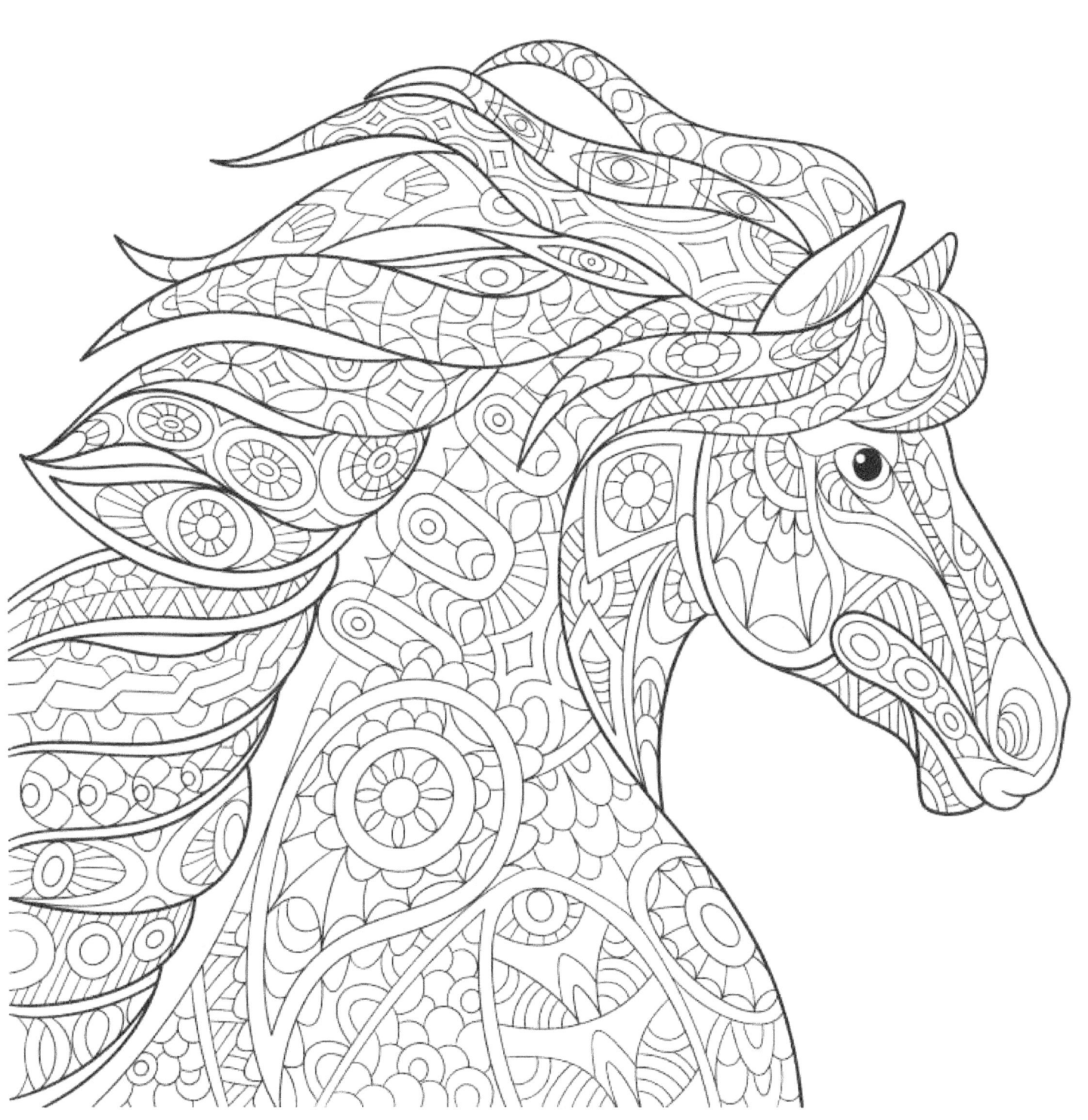

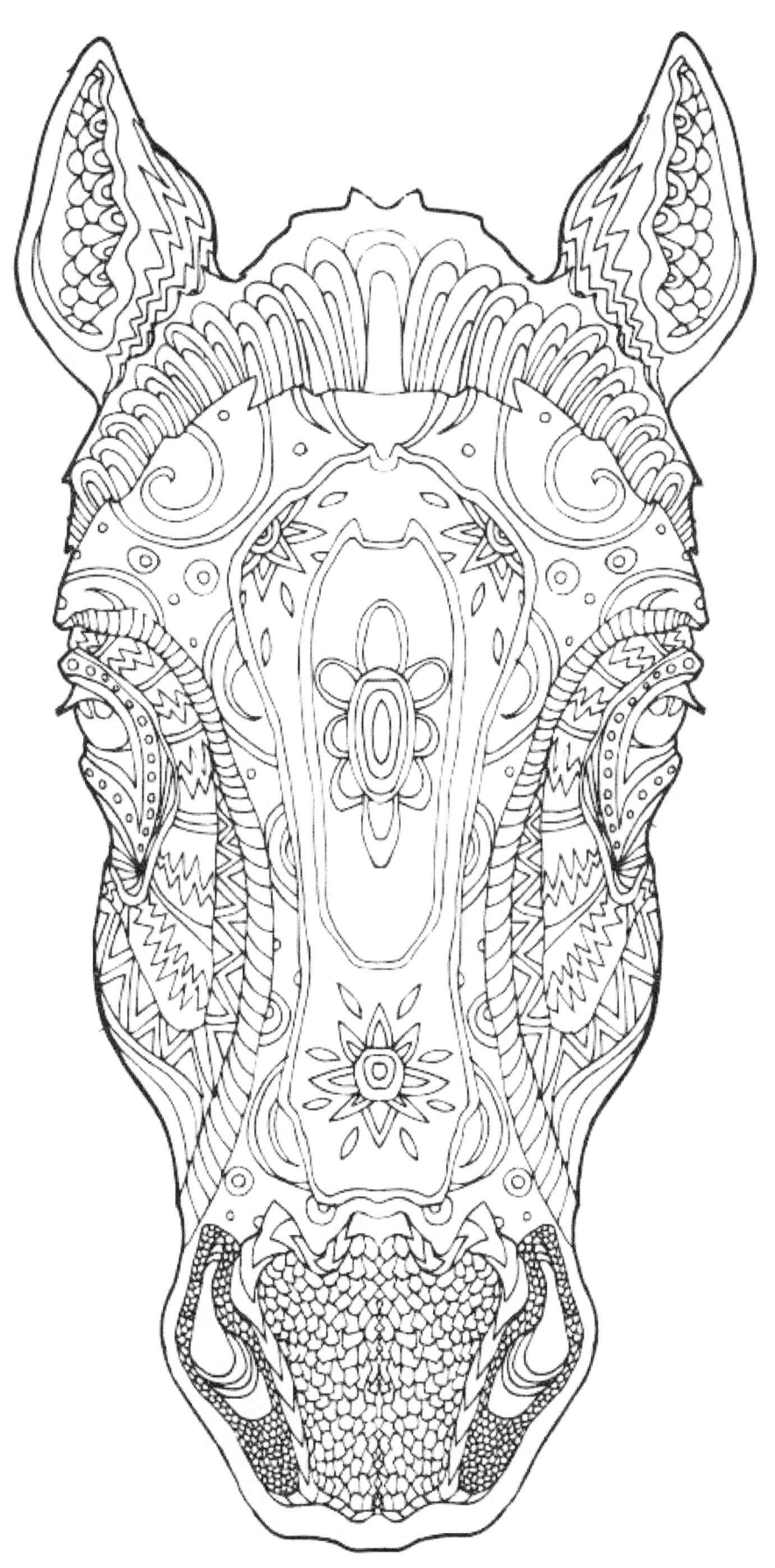

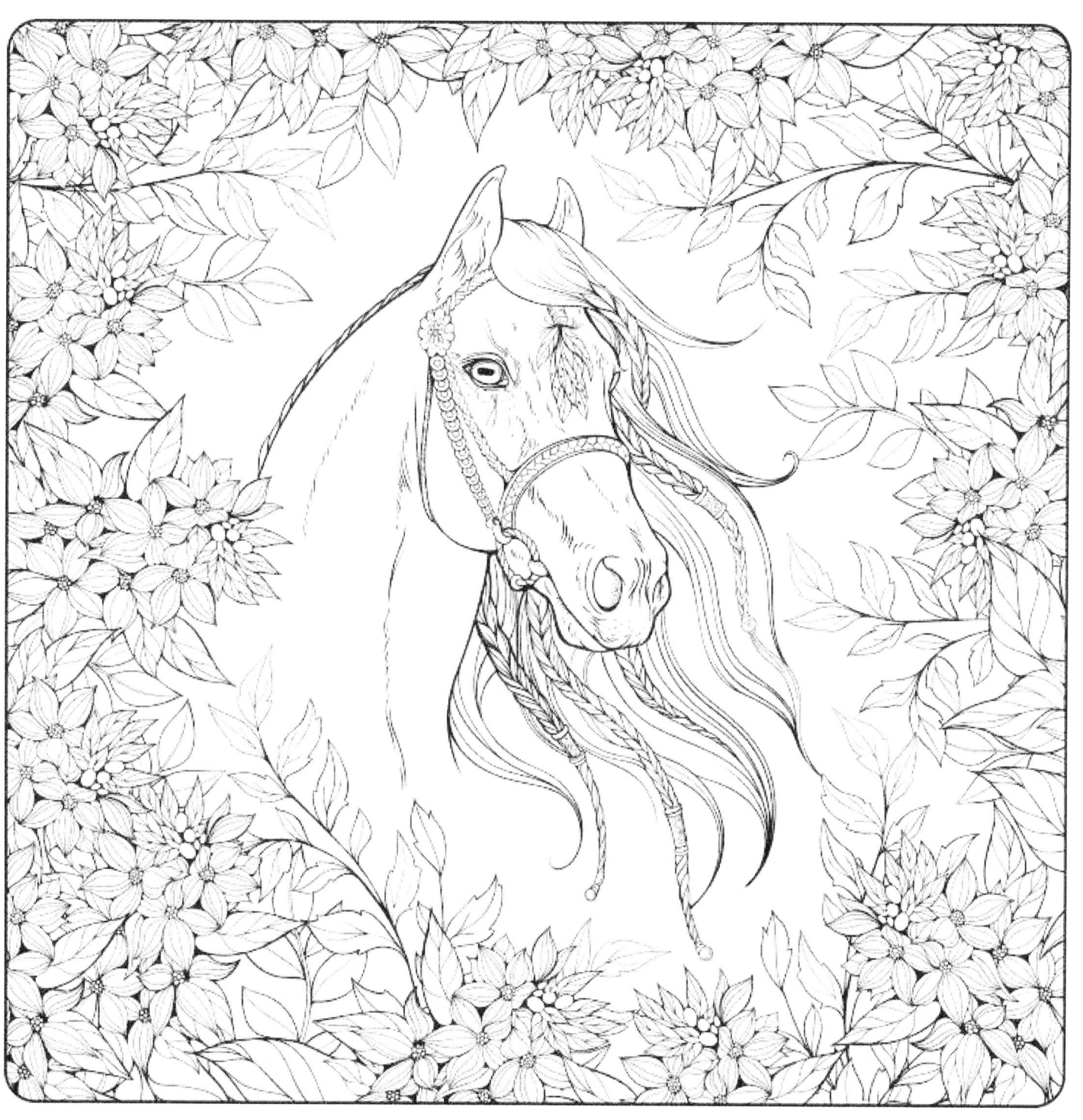

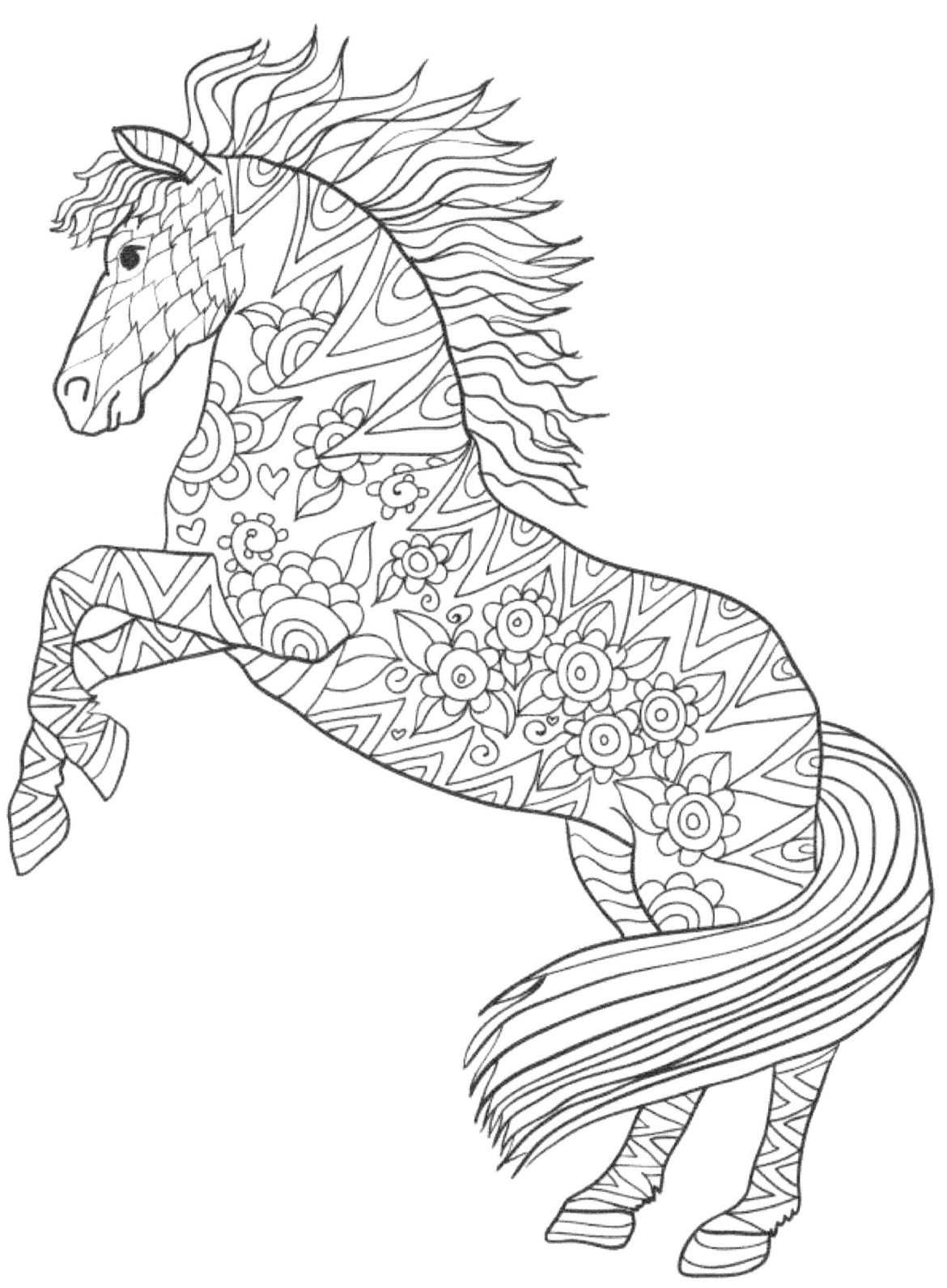

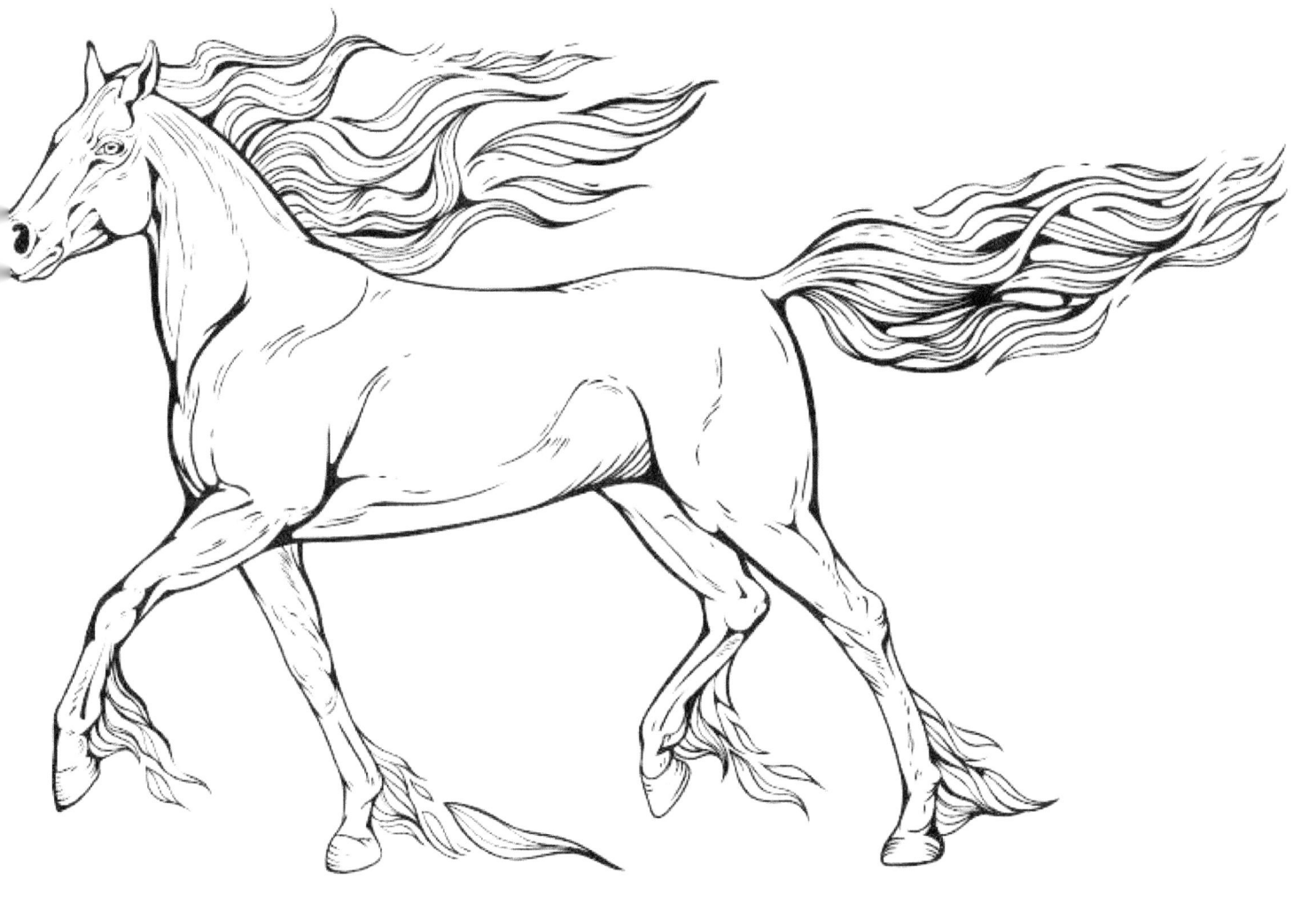

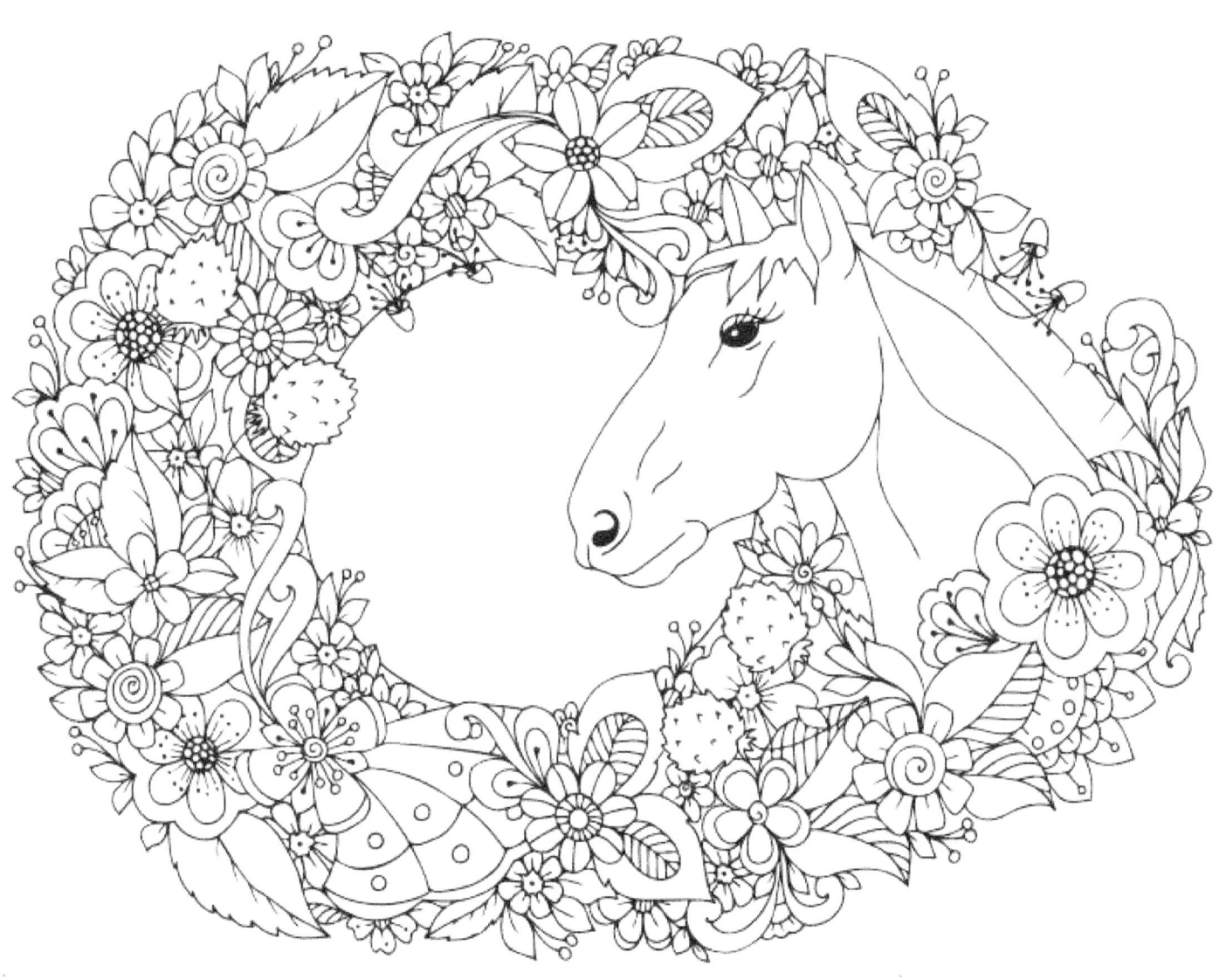

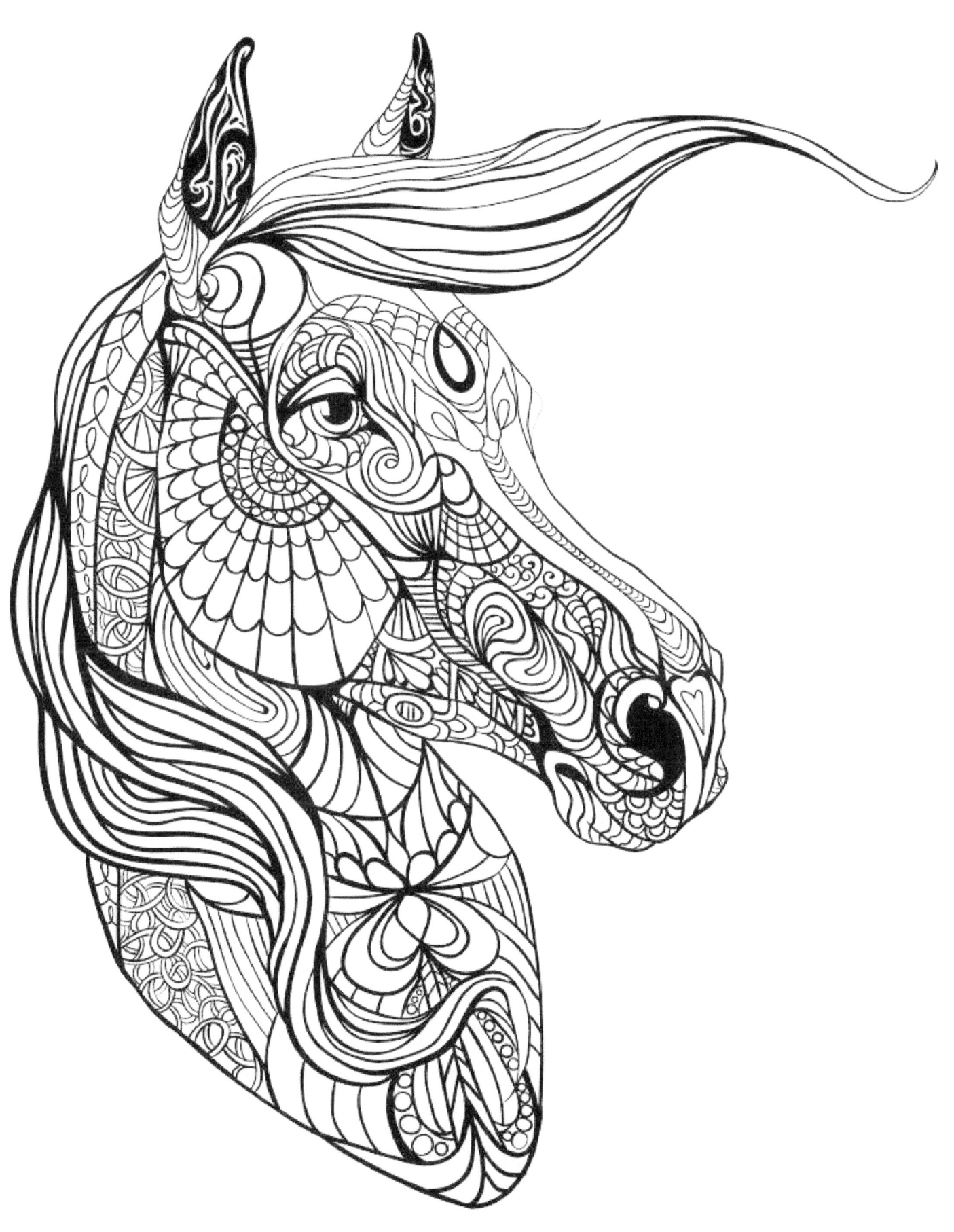

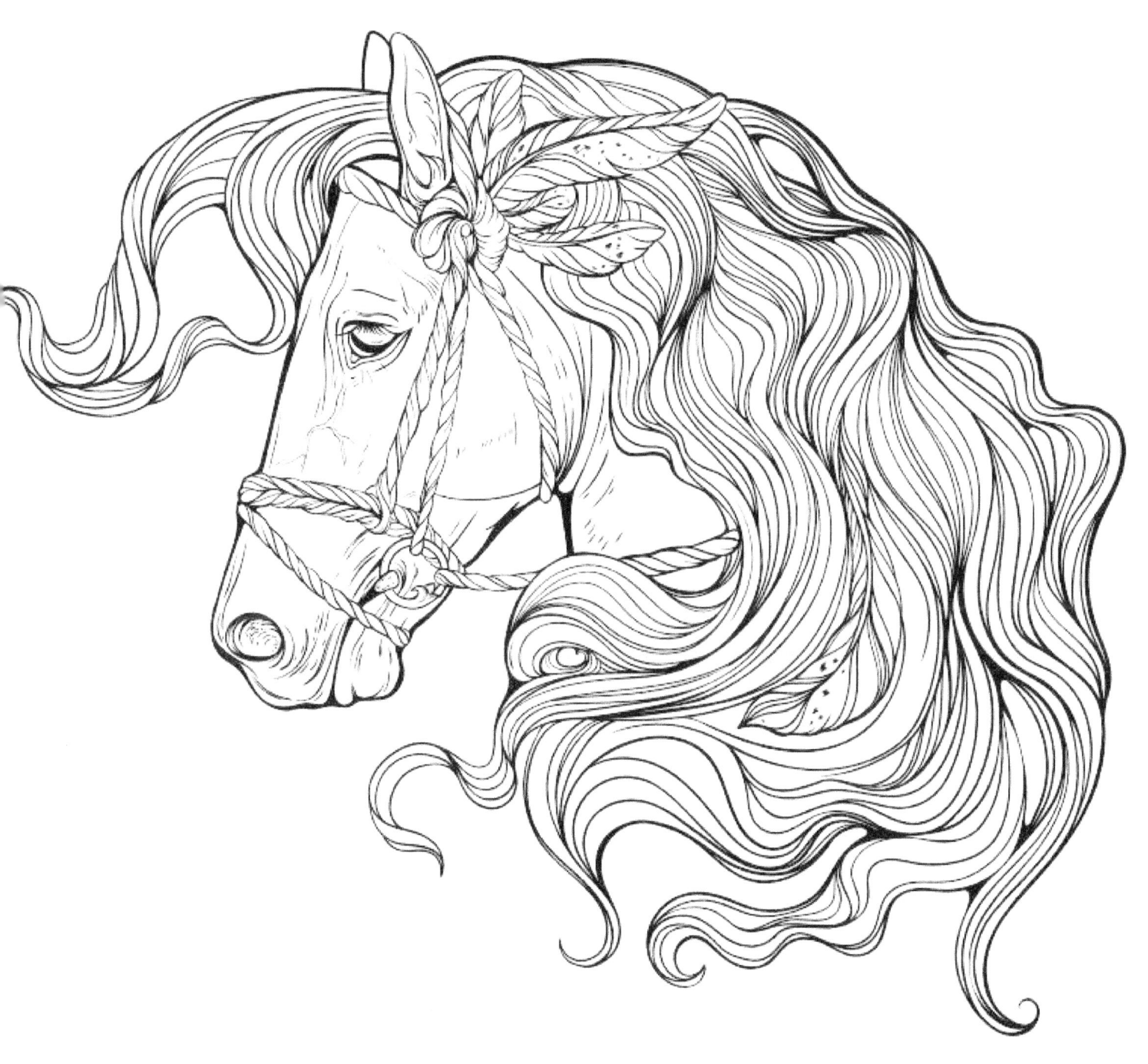

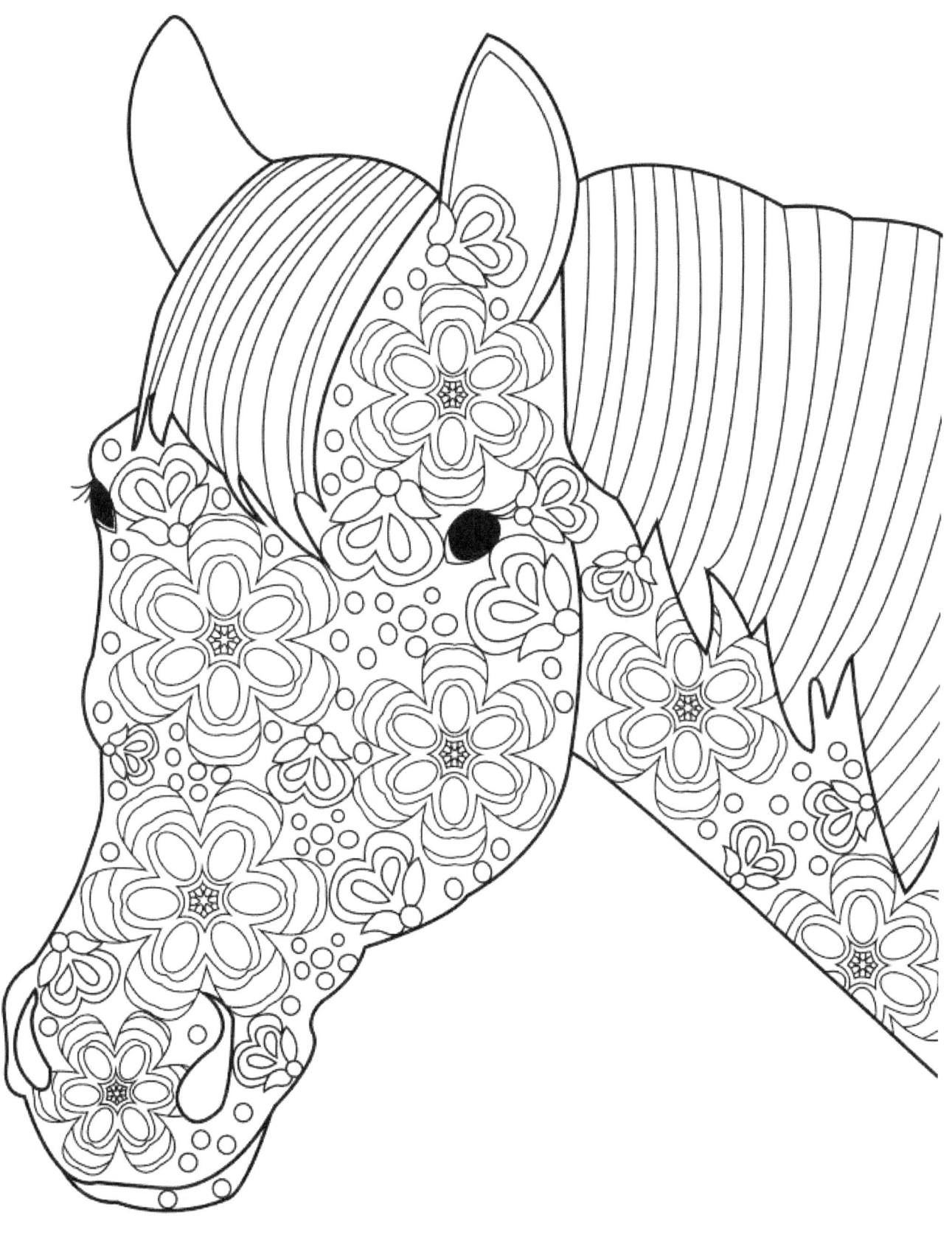

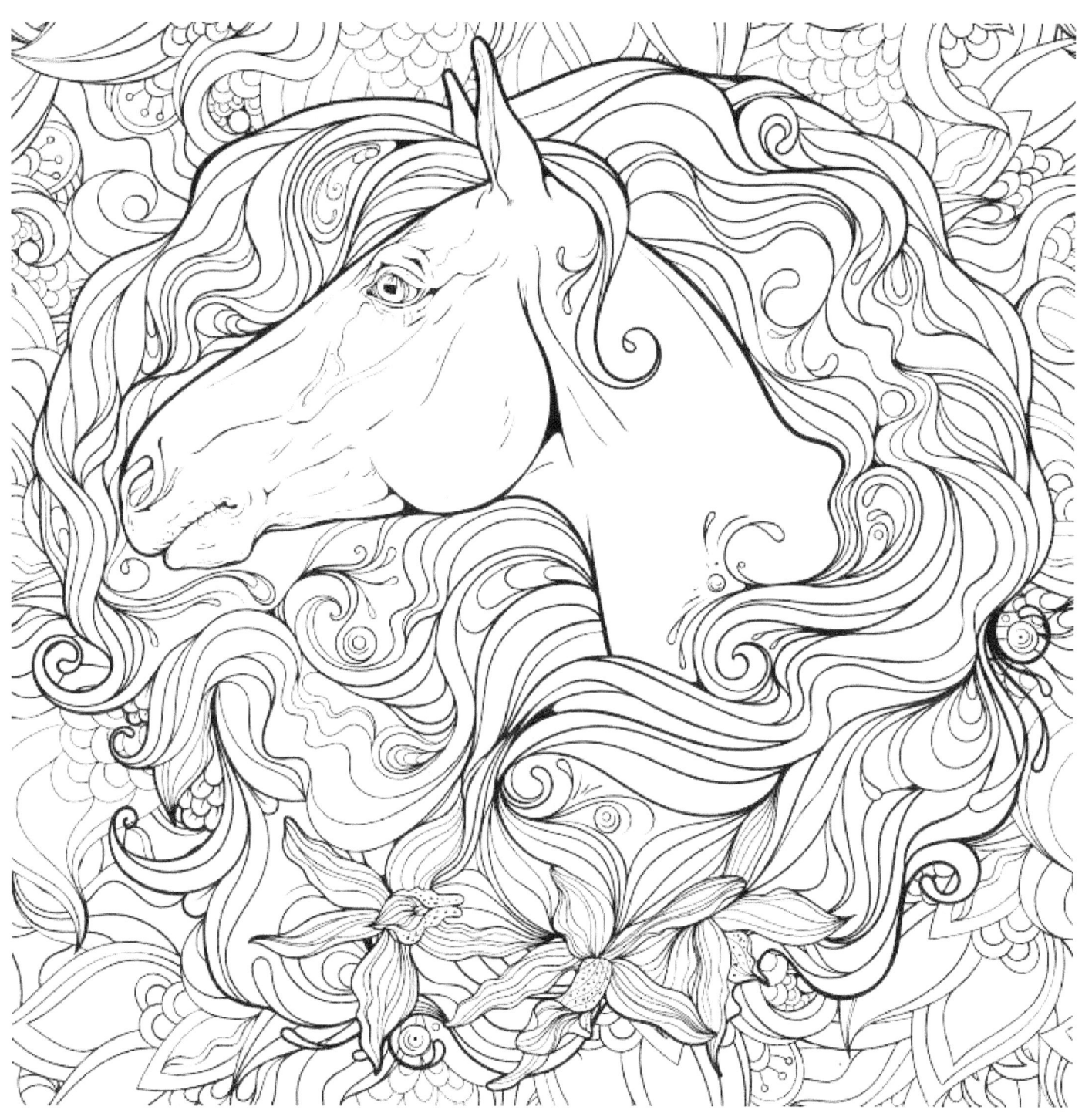

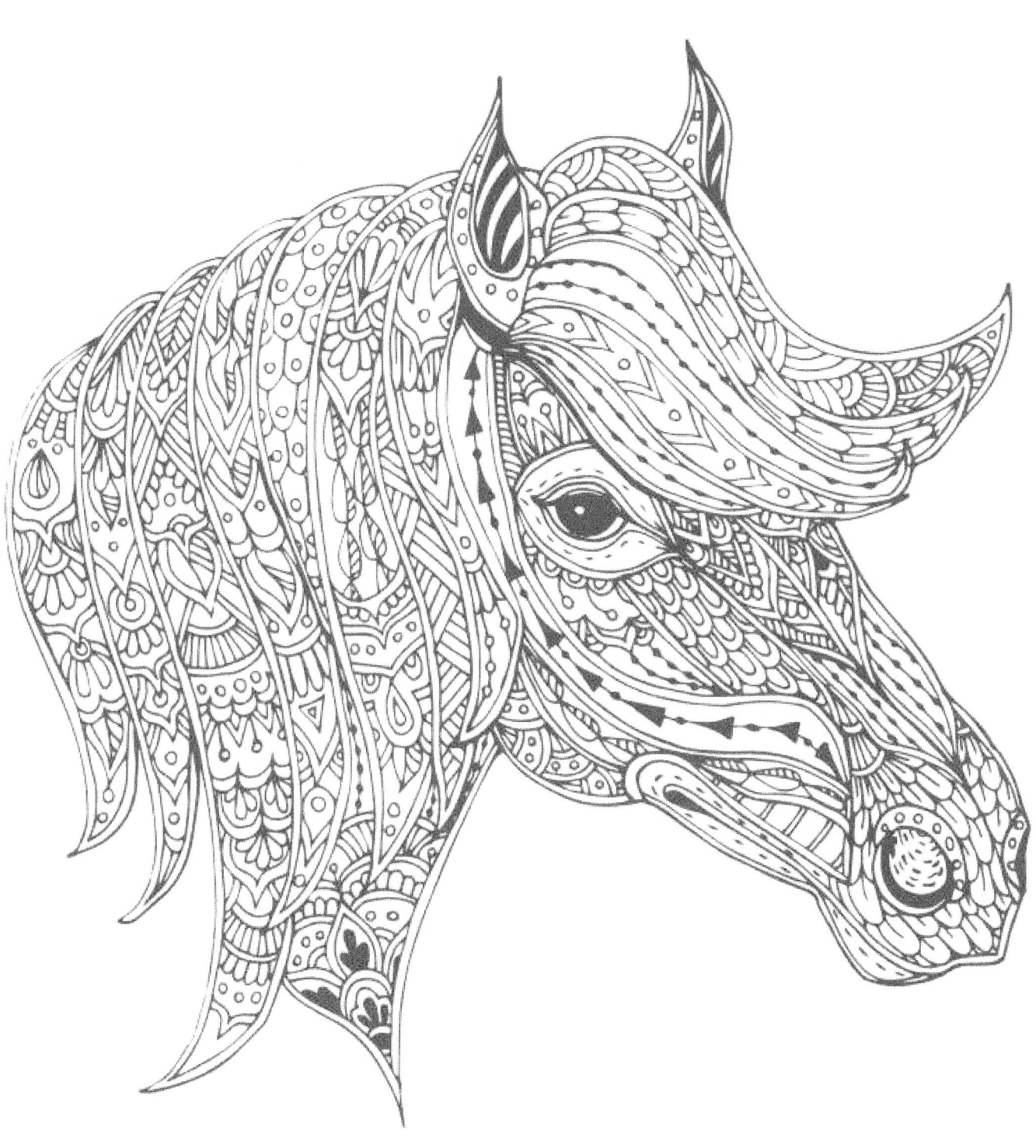

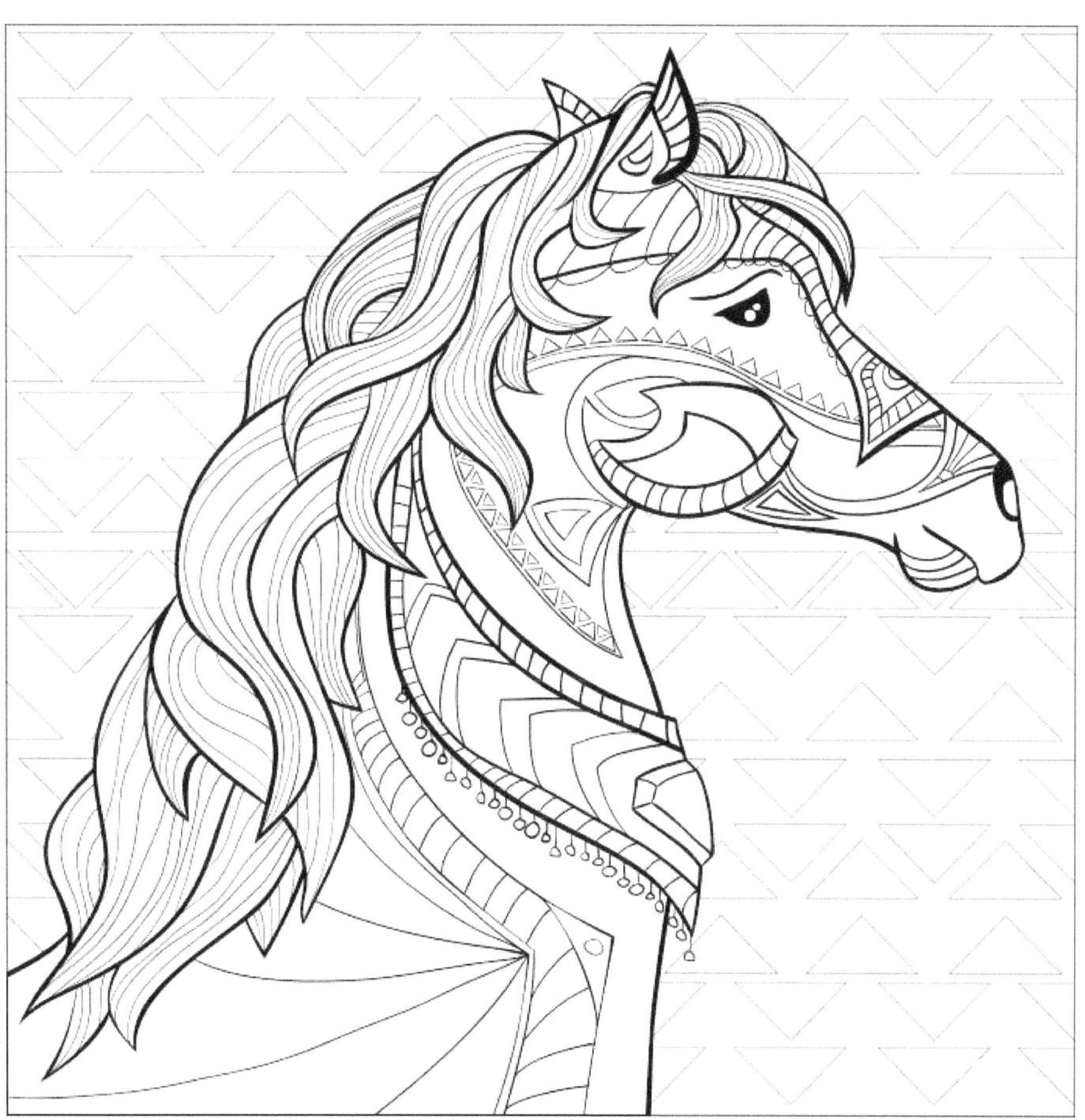

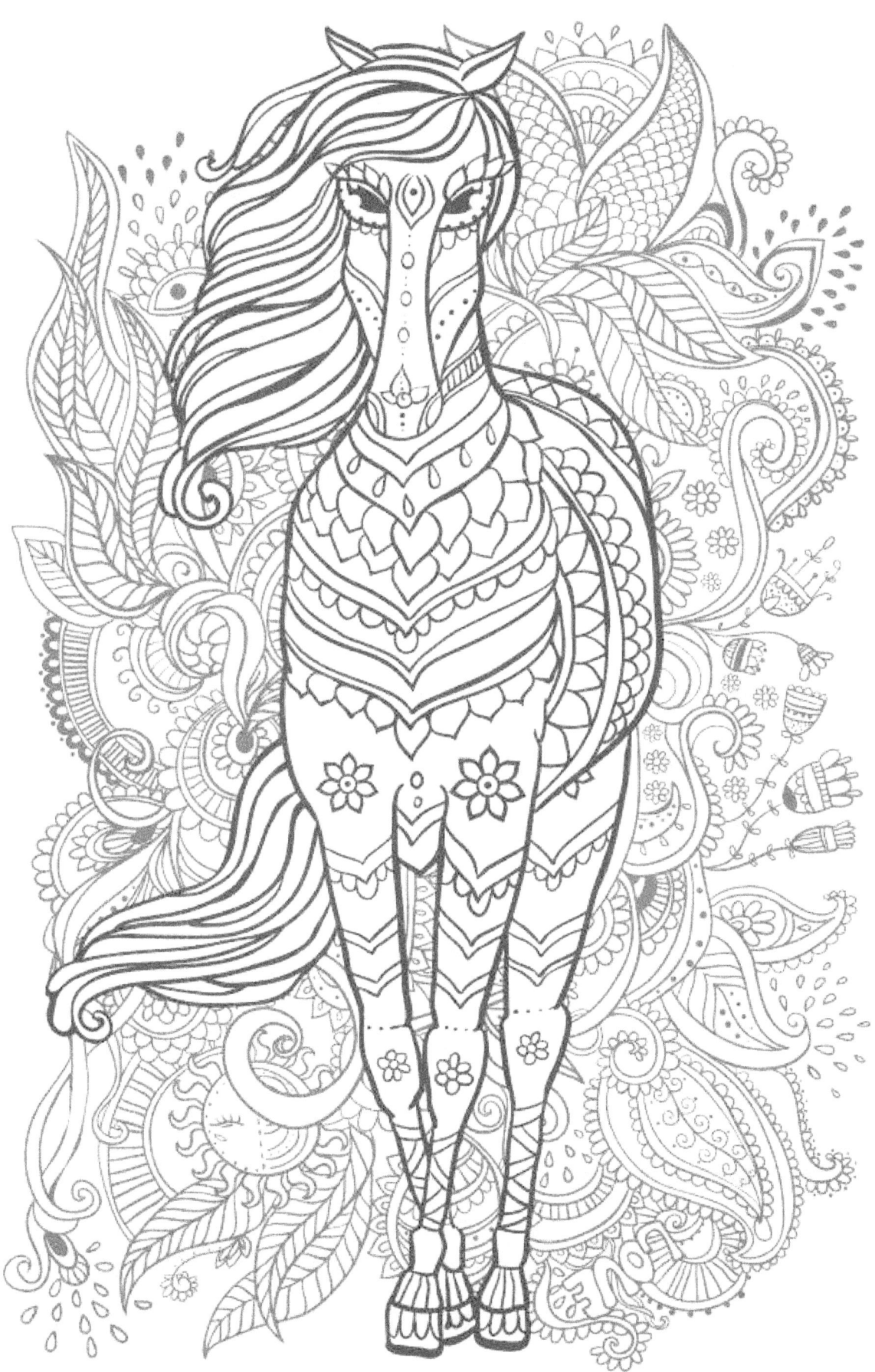

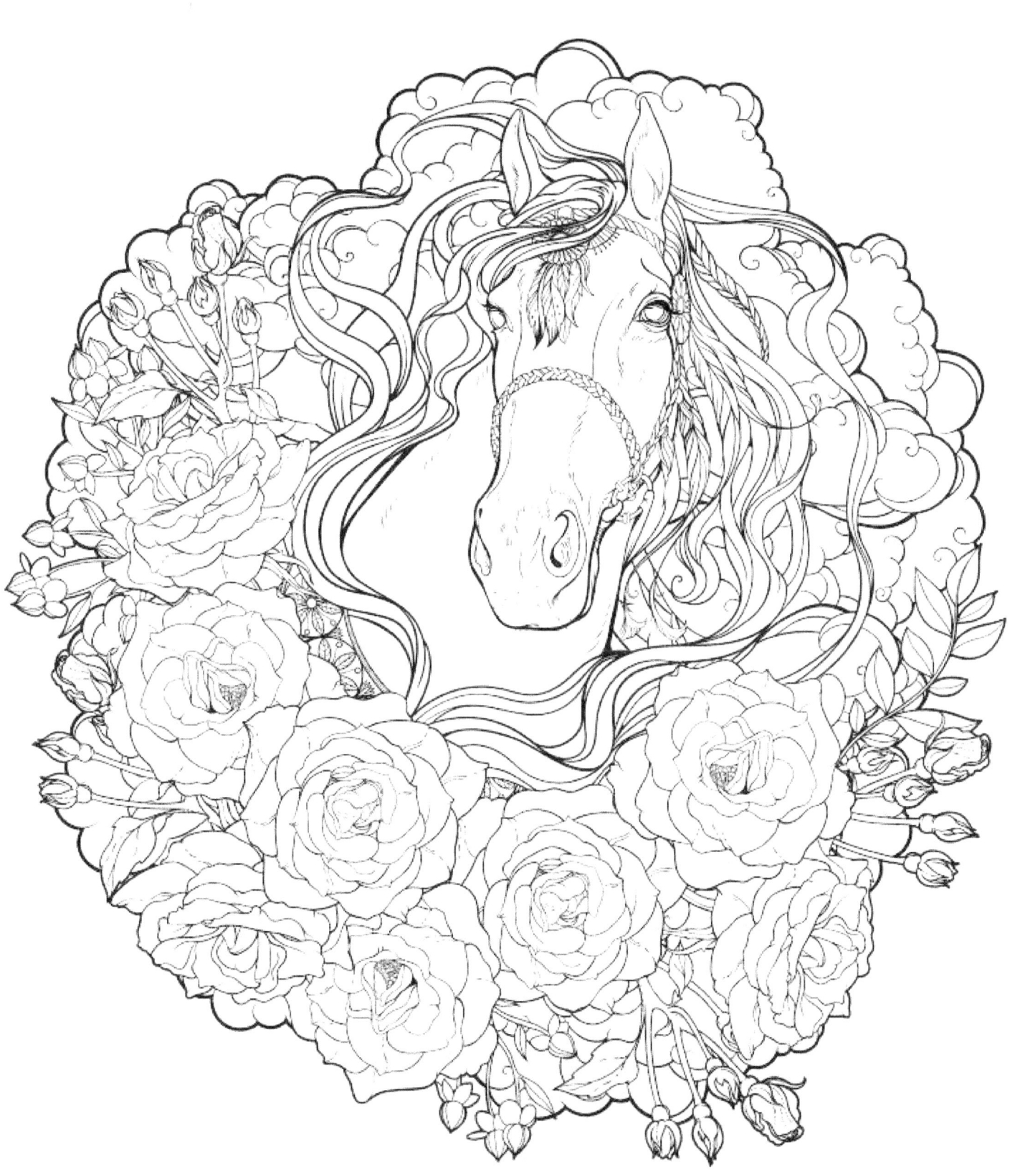

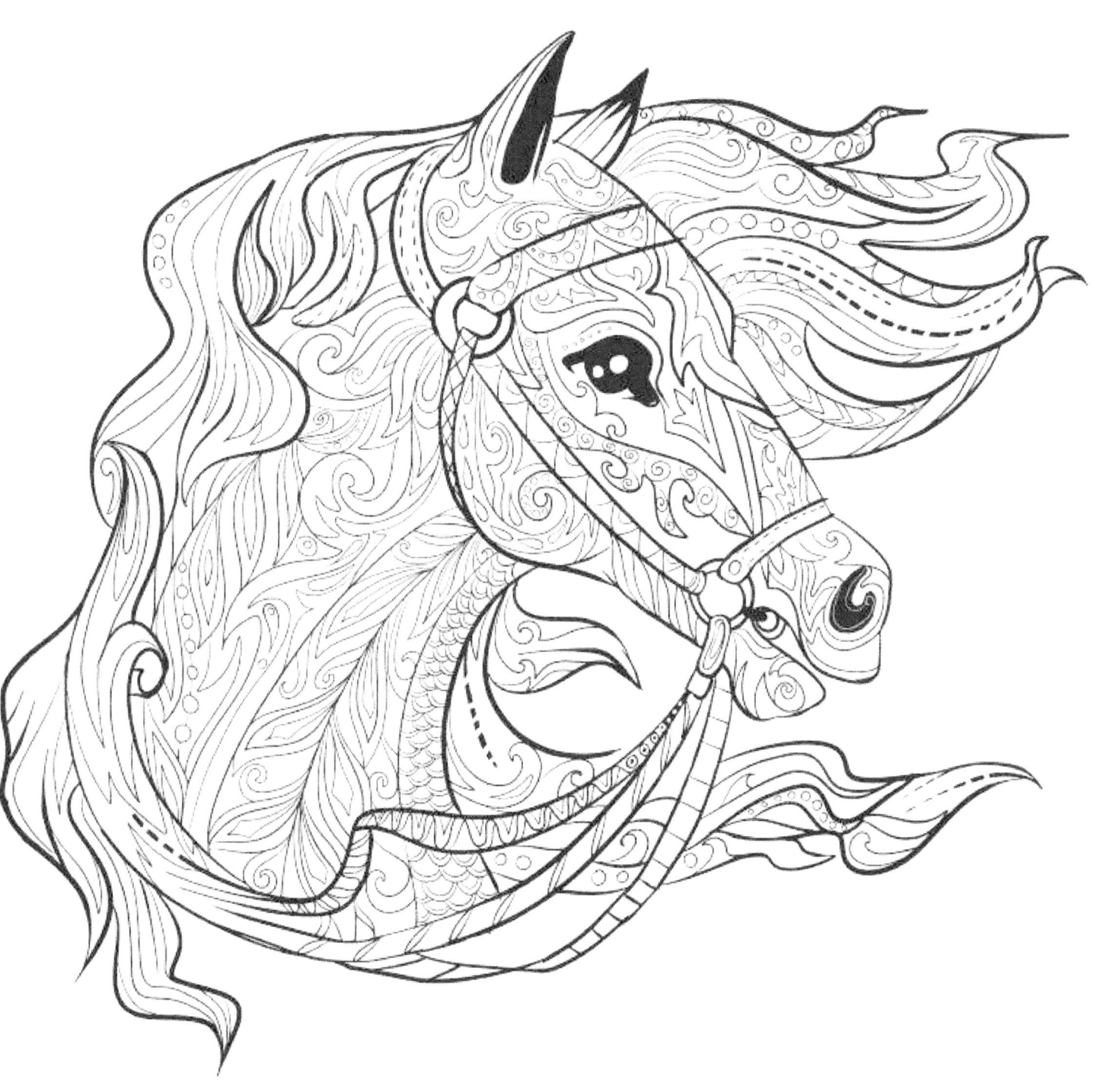

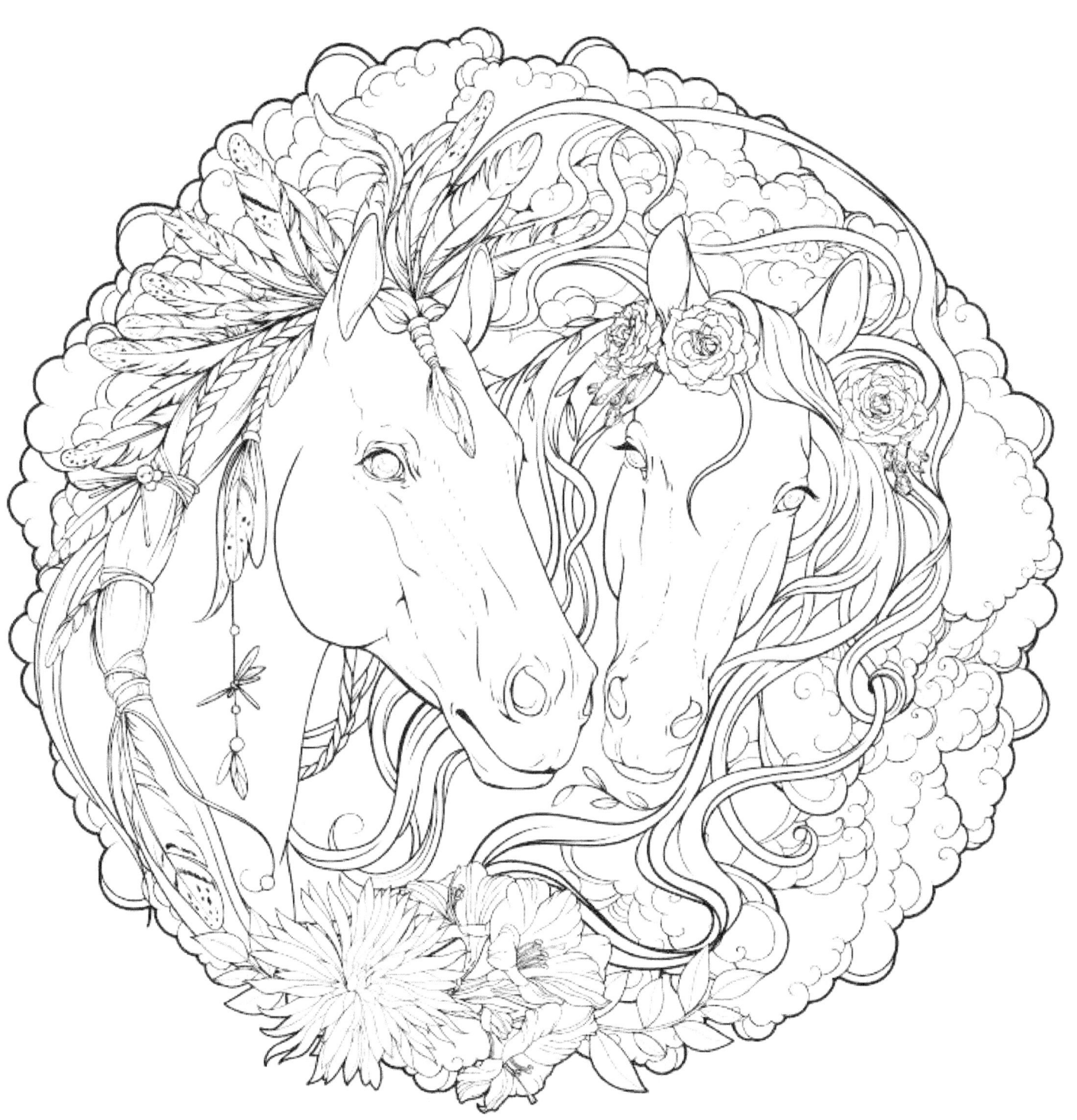

www.ingramcontent.com/pod-product-compliance
Lightning Source LLC
Chambersburg PA
CBHW081157180526
45170CB00006B/2117